BOB WOOLMER ON
BATTING

BOB WOOLMER ON
BATTING

Bob Woolmer

Tim Noakes

with Helen Moffett

NEW HOLLAND

This edition first published in 2010 by New Holland Publishers (UK) Ltd
London • Cape Town • Sydney • Auckland
www.newhollandpublishers.com

Garfield House, 86–88 Edgware Road, London W2 2EA, United Kingdom
Cornelis Struik House, 80 McKenzie Street, Cape Town 8001, South Africa
Unit 1, 66 Gibbes Street, Chatswood, NSW 2067, Australia
218 Lake Road, Northcote, Auckland, New Zealand

New Holland Publishing is a member of Avusa Ltd

Extracted from the title *Bob Woomer's Art and Science of Cricket*

Reproduction by Hirt & Carter Cape (Pty) Ltd
Printed and bound by Replika Press Pvt Ltd, India

10 9 8 7 6 5 4 3 2 1

Publishing Manager: Linda de Villiers
Editor and Content Consultant: Tom Eaton
Designer: Beverley Dodd
Cover Designer: Neal Cobourne
Principal Photographer: Carl Fourie
Bowling Grips Illustrator: James Berrangé
Technical Illustrators: James Berrangé and Martin Jones
Proofreaders: Roxanne Reid, Anthony Sharpe and Joy Clack
Indexer: Dawn Dobbins

ISBN: 978 1 84773 749 6

Front cover image © Hamish Blair/Getty Images
Back cover image © Graham Chadwick/Allsport

The authors gratefully acknowledge permission to use copyrighted material from the following: Kerith Aginsky, Justin Durandt, Gallo Images/Getty Images, Janine Gray, Paul Hurrion, Brian Kantor, Alan Knott, Peter Philpott, Marc Portus, Quintic Consultancy Ltd, Martin Schwellnus and Richard Stretch. It has not been possible to trace all copyright holders.

Please contact the publishers at the above address in case of errors or omissions.

CONTENTS

INTRODUCTION

Of all cricket's skills, batting is the most glamorous. At the highest level of the game, scoring runs and not being dismissed will bring fame and glory of a kind that is possibly unique in the world of sport. In the 1930s, the cricketing world regarded Sir Donald Bradman with the kind of awe reserved for monarchs and film stars; and Brian Lara's 375 against England in 1994 earned him similar status. At the summit of batting achievement lies immense prestige.

But batting is the skill that will also take the most time to learn and perfect. This process begins with understanding the *how* and *why* of the art. Unfortunately, too many coaching manuals still focus on the how without explaining the why.

Batting is difficult, and anyone who walks out to the crease to bat will discover three immediate problems: judging length, judging line, and being able to move properly; or, more specifically, getting balanced to deal with that line and length. Batting in cricket is not a natural movement like slugging a baseball: even a child with good ball skills will struggle to bring bat into contact with the ball, especially if the ball bounces high.

Many young batters aren't exposed to the deviating ball, because young bowlers aren't able to move it off a straight line. When you first set out to bowl, the ball goes straight to the batter. If it does deviate, it's probably doing so into the side of the net! Young bowlers only start being able to spin the ball when they are nine or ten – and if they are able to bowl true leg-spin at that age, it confuses the batsmen completely because they've had little or no experience of such dramatic changes in line.

However, when you move to a higher level of the game, the skills of batting – picking line and length, balance, shot selection, shot execution – have all been mastered and become second nature. At this level, the only thing that keeps batsmen from scoring freely is deviation.

But what of the highest level? Why don't all Test batsmen score triple-hundreds regularly, especially on pitches that don't help the ball to deviate? Here the enemy is almost always mental pressure. It takes more than talent to excel: when Brian Lara took the world record for the highest Test score for the second time (400 not out in April 2004), his effort required immense concentration, application, desire and skill.

Test batsmen are good enough to look for swing, to see the shine on the ball, to look at the finger position at the point of delivery, and to check the angle of the seam. But movement off the seam will always remain a problem, because it happens so fast and so late. If you're facing a Glenn McGrath and you've committed to a particular line, and the ball jags back or away, there just isn't time to adjust. If you're lucky, you'll miss. If not, the scorecard will show J. Bloggs, caught Gilchrist bowled McGrath.

On English wickets of the past decades, a lot of batsmen were able to play a line, see the ball deviate, and adjust in time, because the wicket was slow. But in Australia or South Africa, where pitches tend to be quicker, a batsman may see the ball move, start to adjust, but only have time to get an edge on it and nick off a catch. Sides who tour these countries have to learn to play inside the line of the ball – in other words, not to follow the ball, as they would in countries like India and Pakistan, which generally have slower pitches.

It *is* possible to play the seaming ball. As with all sports, the messages sent to the brain by the eyes dictate how the body will respond, and the response from the body is conditioned by how you've practised or trained yourself. There are days when you find you can play the swinging or seaming ball with ease, when you're so still and balanced that if the ball seams away, you can adjust and hit it through the covers. But there are also days when batting just seems impossible.

When everything does go right, when you're able to play every ball on its merit, and place it just where you want it to go, it is usually the result of being in what sports psychologists call your *ideal performance state*. (Laypeople talk about being in a bubble or 'in the zone'.) And once you are in that state, you become oblivious to everything around you except the ball you are facing. Everything seems to slow down, giving you plenty of time to react.

This is often evident in Tests. Dashing strokemakers such as Chris Gayle or David Gower will keep the bowlers in the game all the time, offering chances. But when batsmen like Ricky Ponting or Sunil Gavaskar enter the zone, bowlers just don't know what to do to get them out. In the end, their only option is to break down that bubble, through verbal intimidation or by distracting them by mixing up the attack.

First, however, it is important to learn enough about the art of batting, especially the how and why of batting, to be able to reach that zone.

THE BASICS OF BATTING

THE PRINCIPLES OF BATTING

In 1851 the Reverend James Pycroft set out six golden rules of batting in *The Cricket Field*. In 1980, England match-winner Ian Botham did the same, proving that 130 years had done nothing to alter the principles of good batsmanship.

	PYCROFT	BOTHAM
1	Sight of a ball depends on a habit of individual attention both before and after delivery.	Concentrate.
2	How characteristic in the ease and repose of their figures – no hurry or trepidation. How little do their heads or bodies move!	Keep your head still and get it over the ball.
3	By standing close up, and playing well over your wicket with straight bat, and throwing, by means of the left leg, the body forwards, over a ball rising to off stump, you can make an effective hit from an off-bailer without lessening your defence.	Get behind the line.
4	One of the best leg hitters is Dakin, and his rule is: keep your right foot firm on the ground: advance the left straight at the pitch, and as far as you can reach, and hit as straight at the pitch as you can.	Get your foot to the ball when you play forward.
5	The bat, though properly 4½ inches wide, is considerably reduced when used across the wicket: *so never hit across the wicket.*	Bring the bat through straight.
6	Let your arms do the hitting.	Extend the arms when you play shots.

SOURCE: SYNGE AND ANNS, 1987, P. 115

Coaches and commentators talk about sticking to the basics, but what does this actually mean? As illustrated, both Botham and Pycroft, 130-odd years apart in time, identified six basic aspects of batting that they believed to be vital. It is perhaps simpler to cut this list down to five basic principles. If these are adhered to, they will give all batsmen the best possible chance of succeeding at the highest level.

These five basic principles of batting are:

1. Watch the ball.
2. Keep your head still on release of the ball.
3. Judge length accurately: line will change with swing and spin.
4. Allow your hands to lead your body and feet into the correct position.
5. Select the correct shot.

THE SCIENCE OF BATTING

Batting is a science, one that uses a number of skills:

- *Visual and neurological skills* – watching the ball, judging where it goes, processing this information (a lightning-swift unconscious process), decision-making and shot-selection.
- *Physical and biomechanical skills* – creating the correct body movements so that shot-making corresponds with the length and line of the ball, timing the hitting of the ball.
- *Psychological skills* – dealing with the elation and depression associated with scoring a hundred or a duck.

On a more practical and step-by-step level, the skill of batting requires the batsman to watch the ball from the bowler's hand, judge where it is likely to pitch, move the feet and body into position to hit it, and then choose the correct shot to either score or survive. All this while the ball travels in excess of 140km per hour, leaving the batter 0.4 of a second to respond to a hard leather ball weighing 156 grams, a missile that can break bones – and even kill.

This is why a batsman's courage (and his luck) can determine success or failure. However, no top batsman relies on courage and luck: he relies on his technique, and his understanding of what he does, and when and why he does it.

1. WATCH THE BALL

The eyes will give the brain the first clues as to where the delivery is going to land and therefore start your decision-making process. So when should you start watching the ball? This differs from batsman to batsman; however, the pre-delivery clues are often there if you know where to look for them.

How early a batsman starts watching the ball (during the bowler's run-up, during his gather) is a matter of personal preference, but it is vital that you are watching the ball as it leaves the bowler's hand: look for the shine, the position of the seam, what the fingers do and where it is released. The release position determines the length of the delivery, and being able to use visual clues will help you to decide (correctly!) whether to go forward or back. For example, some bowlers hold the ball deep in their fingers – almost against their palm – when bowling a slower ball, while Shane Warne's flipper was held in the end of his fingers.

2. KEEP YOUR HEAD STILL – BE BALANCED

> *Stand up as straight as possible, too. If you crouch… and then have to straighten up as you play the ball, your eyes will be on a different plane, and you will look at the ball from a changing angle, just when you need concentration most. Imagine a rifleman moving his head up as he fires, and you will see what I mean. You should keep your eyes at the same height from the ground right through the shot, whether with bat or gun, if it is accuracy you want.*
>
> Learie Constantine, *The Changing Face of Cricket*

Despite being over half a century old, this advice from one of the masters of early West Indian cricket is still absolutely correct: all coaches will implore a batsman to stand still when the ball is released, and indeed to remain still for up to 2/100ths of a millisecond afterwards. A motionless head means your eyes can focus on the ball, and this will enable you to see where it is going and where it will land. The reflex action that follows – reflex because it has been drummed into you through practice and repetition – will be more precise as a result.

Against great fast bowlers, a batsman often doesn't have time to get properly balanced or become entirely still as the ball is delivered. He needs a quick reflex movement to get him ready, both physically and mentally, to play the correct shot. This movement creates a batting rhythm, which helps him get into an advanced position to deal with the ball landing in a particular area (an area which is often only guessed at – or hoped for!). If the ball is not in that area, he can easily transfer his body into a second position. For example, his first movement could prepare him

NOW YOU SEE IT, NOW YOU DON'T

The question of vision and the role it plays in batting is the new frontier in sports medicine and cricket science. New research is fuelling and stimulating debate over whether batters are actually watching the ball (in a strictly physiological sense) all the way out of the bowler's hand down to the pitch. There are indications that in fact the eye/brain connection makes a lightning-swift and involuntary jump from the bowler's hand to where the batter's brain estimates the ball is most likely to pitch. This information is particularly important for coaches, as well as batters who like to understand every aspect of their game. As this fascinating new material falls somewhere between physiology and the technique of 'watching the ball', we have included it in a separate chapter on 'Vision and Batting' on p. 100–119. For now, however, concentrate on watching the ball with unwavering focus.

for short deliveries, but still enable the fallback option of transferring his weight forwards, allowing him to deal more quickly with fuller deliveries.

This pre-delivery movement is known as a rhythm or trigger movement. When playing in the Asian subcontinent, where pitches are slower and batsmen have more time to react, trigger movements can become more of a shuffle. Pre-delivery movements are discussed in more detail on pp. 34–8.

3. JUDGE LENGTH

It's an all-too-common exchange:

Coach: 'What happened there?'
Player: 'It kept low, coach.'
Coach: 'Don't you think you might have gone forward?'

The player walks off in a huff, but fortunately, with more video analysis available, coaches are able to win these kinds of arguments by proving to their players that they were going through their trigger movements as the ball was on the way down to them. In other words, the batsman hadn't decided yet whether to go forward or back.

It may seem obvious, but for a batsman to be successful, he has to be able to make the correct decision: going forward to a bouncer or back to a half-volley leads inevitably to dismissal, not to mention embarrassment or even injury. The short ball aimed at the chest and above will bounce too high for a comfortable and controlled forward shot, and the ball will either hit the glove or the body, leading either to a catch in the gully region or injury. Going back to a ball of good length or a half-volley will cause the ball to rush onto the batsman, beating his hurried defensive adjustments, and he will be bowled or out LBW. This is what made Warne's flipper so lethal: its flight and top-spin persuaded batsmen to play back, expecting a long-hop, only to have the ball skid onto them and trap them LBW.

In short, being able to move forward and back correctly greatly increases the chances of success; therefore early and accurate judging of length becomes vital.

4. MOVE INTO THE CORRECT POSITION

Coaches always talk about getting the feet into the correct position, but they should really include the hands and the body in that statement: the feet may move, but other parts of the body don't always go where they should! For example, when playing forward, the head, front shoulder and foot should move together, either in line with the ball when defending, or next to the ball when attacking.

Of course, a batsman can still score runs if his feet are in the wrong position, and many players have swung wildly and been effective: we've all seen tail-enders get away with murder. However, as in any racket or ball sport, it is better to get the feet moving correctly, as balance and a good base will make sure that the shot is correctly executed.

Good footwork simply aids good balance. To illustrate how body mechanics work, and how big a stride you really need when playing forward, try the following exercise: stand with your feet together, arms folded across your chest. Now lean sideways towards the point on the pitch (or the carpet) where the bowler would be aiming, until you are about to topple over. Notice just how far your front leg has to move to prevent you from falling and restore your balance.

Batting is essentially a sideways game, played along parallel lines. The ball travels on one line and the bat should meet the ball on that line. This means that the body should therefore travel along a parallel line next to the ball. Whether or not this happens depends almost entirely on getting the feet into the correct position.

To make sure that this particular point is clear, think carefully about what terminology you use. Bob Woolmer said he always cringed when hearing coaches yell, 'Get your foot to the pitch of the ball!', as this would imply that the batsman should get his foot to exactly where the ball pitches. This of course is a total misnomer, as following this instruction would mean the ball bouncing on the batsman's instep!

There are two basic points to remember when playing forward:

- when attacking, get beside the ball and give yourself room to hit it;
- when defending, get your head, front shoulder and foot into line with the ball.

PITCH-PERFECT SHOT SELECTION

The condition of the pitch often dictates shot selection, but what are these conditions? Slow pitches, pitches with uneven bounce, fast pitches – what distinguishes each one, and how do they affect batting?

When discussing shot selection, it is important to cover the basic differences in pitch conditions. A slow pitch is one on which the ball grips as it pitches, either because the pitch is wet and soft, or dry and dusty (sometimes even crumbling, as is often the case in Asia). On such pitches, a 120km/h delivery can slow down to around 105km/h on contact, while on a fast pitch (whether hard-rolled clay, as at Sabina Park in the 1980s, or a slippery green-top like the Wanderers in the same decade), the ball arrives at the batsman's end apparently as quickly as it left the bowler's hand. While there is minuscule deceleration due to friction, to the batsman, the difference is negligible.

This apparent speed off the pitch is described as the ball 'coming onto the bat' or 'sliding on', and is largely a product of the batsman's reflexes: by the time the ball pitches, the batsman has already made a prediction as to how fast the ball is 'coming on' to him, and has already started to swing the bat in anticipation of the ball's arrival. If his prediction is wrong, and he swings too early, the chances are that he will claim that the pitch is slow and is 'holding' the ball back. However, if the deceleration of the ball is minimal, or he's reading the pitch well and his prediction is good, he'll find he has time to select the correct shot, and time it well.

But international batsmen can't allow themselves to be restricted by pitches that don't seem to 'come on', and so they learn to play differently on different surfaces. No two countries share identical soil conditions, or indeed conditions such as humidity, cloud cover and dampness, all of which affect swing and seam.

It is therefore important to have practised a wide range of shots for all conditions, and then to choose the appropriate shots for each ball and each surface.

5. SELECT THE CORRECT SHOT

Peter May, the brilliant batsman who dominated English cricket during the 1950s, said that for every question the bowler asks the batsman, there is an answer. In other words, for every type of delivery, there is a correct shot. Whether or not you get the answer right depends on how well you have trained yourself to respond automatically.

Of course, some players are so good that they no longer need to provide orthodox answers to the bowlers' questions. The two Richards, Viv and Barry, were among the exceptionally gifted batsmen who could hit the ball wherever they wanted: a half-volley a foot outside off stump would normally go through the covers, but Sir Viv was just as likely to plant it between mid-wicket and square leg, such was his ability.

But for those not blessed with such superhuman gifts, scoring runs is much easier if you have the necessary options to deal with the variety of positions in which the ball lands. The more shots you have – and the more you are 'grooved' to pull out the right shot for the right ball in the right conditions – the better off you will be.

Field settings also control shot selection. If a batsman is limited in his array of shots, it allows the opposition to bowl to a set field. This often causes frustration that ultimately leads to a rash shot and dismissal. Good captains and bowlers will quickly notice any weakness in a batsman's array of shots or defensive technique and exploit it in this way.

WRAPPING UP THE BIG FIVE

The five principles of batting outlined above are the cornerstone of a successful career as a batsman. These techniques must be learnt and practised until they enter the subconscious and become reflex actions. This kind of conditioning takes time – between seven and ten years, depending on how hard and often the individual practises. But by the end of that time, reactions will be instant – known as 'grooved'.

TIMING THE BALL: CRICKET IS A TWO-HANDED GAME

'Woolmer! You're using too much bottom hand!'

Many batsmen will have heard a similar cry from their coach. Unfortunately, this debate doesn't usually go much further: as a young player, Bob Woolmer was often tempted to reply, 'All right then, tell me how you want me to use my bottom hand!'

The problem is not so much 'too much' bottom hand as incorrect use of the bottom hand. Over the years, coaches have neglected the importance of the use of the bottom hand. Bob Woolmer recounted: 'I asked a group of 50 coaches to raise their hands if they thought batting was controlled by the top hand: almost all raised a hand. I then asked them to think about the drill of hitting high catches for fielding practice: which hand did they use? Top or bottom? All answered that they used the bottom hand. And so I asked them again: which hand controls the shot? The debate started afresh!'

Batting is two-handed, like golf and hockey. However, everyone has a dominant hand (90% of people are right-hand dominant), which is most clearly evident when they throw or write or play one-handed games like tennis. It is this dominant hand that provides the power and timing while batting.

In baseball, or when playing a two-handed tennis shot, hand dominance is not a problem: both a home-run to left field and a cross-court backhand winner use simple biomechanics, with the waist and shoulders turning as the arms swing across the body. It doesn't matter if either hand comes off the bat or racquet after impact: indeed, in both sports the shot will remain effective if played one-handed, with either hand – only the power of the shot will be affected.

But the shape of the cricket bat forces the batsman to swing his arms in a pendulum movement, thereby forcing the hands and arms to work together. Both hands have separate axes (our shoulders), and so they have different swing planes, separated by a distance of anything up to 80cm, depending on how broad the shoulders are. For example, your left arm can swing out in line with your left shoulder at 90 degrees, but try to swing your right arm out in line with your left shoulder at 90 degrees, and suddenly your chest gets in the way.

A bat held with two hands together will hang immediately under your eyes, and in a direct line down the centre of the body. But this vertical position is the only time on the bat's pendulum swing path that the two hands will be in equilibrium: before impact it is natural for the top hand to lead the bat, while the untrained batsman will want to use his bottom hand on impact.

This would not be a problem if our arms swung on the same axes, but because the bottom hand is swinging on a different axis to the top hand – and is usually stronger and more co-ordinated – it can destroy the top hand's direction at the crucial moment of impact.

This is what coaches have warned against for generations. But by turning the bottom hand into a bogeyman, they have also overlooked a simple biomechanical principle: the top hand starts the shot on the backswing, and the bottom hand finishes the shot (first with impact, then with follow-through).

In other words, it is the bottom hand that completes the shot and creates both timing and power.

It might be useful to visualize the path of the swing as resembling the hull of a 19th-century man-of-war boat. The backswing towards the stumps is the high bridge and captain's cabin; the hitting area is the flat bottom; and the follow-through is the prow of the boat. It follows

FIGURE 1 *The path followed by the swinging bat*

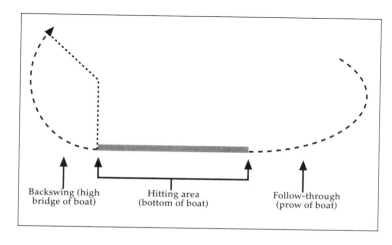

Backswing (high bridge of boat) Hitting area (bottom of boat) Follow-through (prow of boat)

logically that the longer the 'bottom of the boat', the greater the contact point and hitting area will be. The follow-through begins once both hands have travelled along the 'bottom of the boat' for as long as it is physically possible to do so, and then begin lifting because the bottom hand (attached to the back arm) can no longer match the top hand's swing path.

Another way of imagining a successful stroke through the hitting area is to visualize attaching a paintbrush to the end of your bat, and then trying to paint a straight white line while leaning forward into the front-foot drive position. The longer and straighter the line, the better the hitting area.

There is of course no denying that in many players – in some cases, even at international level – the bottom hand influences the top in a negative way, either taking the bat across the line of the delivery, or overtaking the top hand when driving (which will usually induce errors such as missing the ball or scooping it into the air for an easy catch). The bottom hand will also rotate according to its natural biomechanics: if it cannot reach the ball on the bounce, the hand tries to compensate in order to keep the ball down and starts to turn over (the palm rolls down towards the ground). This movement will of course prevent the full face of the bat making contact, and sometimes guarantees a fresh-air shot, much to the batsman's chagrin and the fielders' amusement.

But instead of issuing vague warnings about the dangers of the bottom hand, coaches must recognize that the dominant hand is not going to go away, and that more attention therefore needs to be given to teaching the bottom or dominant hand to work correctly along straight lines.

In summary, always remember that both hands must trace the same path. Wherever the ball goes, both hands must follow it.

LEFT OR RIGHT, TOP OR BOTTOM?

Some batsmen who are generally right-handed, but who have been taught to bat left-handed, find themselves struggling to pull and cut.

Diagnosing this problem once again concerns the bottom hand: the right-handed 'left-hander' sometimes struggles to pull or cut because his bottom hand – in this case his left hand – is not his dominant hand, and is weaker than his right hand. For batsmen with this problem, the pull shot will have to be timed rather than powered. The same applies to right-handed batsmen whose left arm and hand are stronger. Weight training and specific training drills can also improve the strength and co-ordination of the weaker hand.

Former England opener Nick Knight is a good example of a right-handed left-hander: left-handed at the crease, but right-handed at everything else. He hated sweeping, which was natural, as his bottom hand was not the dominant hand; but as soon as he tried reverse sweeping, he found it easier and became extremely successful at this shot. This was not surprising, given that he was now using his dominant hand to hit the ball.

TIMING IS EVERYTHING – CHOOSING A BAT FOR YOUR CHILD

If your child announces that he (or she) hates batting and wants to give up cricket, don't automatically assume it's because of bad coaching or unpleasant teammates. The chances are he's miserable because he's too weak to lift the bat you've given him!

Alarming statistics have shown that the upper body strength of South African children has decreased by over 50% in the last ten years. To investigate this claim, a Western Cape high school known for its cricket conducted a long-term series of tests, and found even more startling results. In 1990, 80% of their under-14 boys tested could do ten or more pull-ups. In 2004, only 10% of them could do one or more pull-up!

As physical education becomes less and less of a priority in South Africa and a growing number of countries around the globe, and as sedentary childhoods revolving around PlayStations and junk food become more prevalent, these statistics are going to get worse.

Of course, children aren't helped by the cost-cutting tactics of their parents. It's an almost universal excuse: the boy's only nine, he's growing like a weed, there's no way I'm spending hundreds of pounds or dollars (or thousands of rands) on something he'll outgrow in a year! The result? Small boys are given bats half as tall as they are, that they have no chance of swinging, let alone learning to play controlled shots with.

The ideal length for a bat is the inside measurement of the batsman's trousers, regardless of whether he is 3 feet or 6 foot 5 inches tall. Bats that come up to a boy's hip or waist will do irreparable damage to his technique – not to mention his pleasure and interest in the game.

The weight of the bat must also be carefully considered. Naturally, some children are stronger than others, but as a general rule of thumb, children over the age of seven fare best with bats that weigh no more than a kilogram. A good yardstick is to ask the child to lift the bat in his non-dominant hand (i.e., his left hand if he is right-handed), and to hold if out horizontally with his shoulder for one minute. If he can do this without strain or difficulty, the weight is correct. Exactly the same precautions apply when choosing bats for girls.

Finally, look for the grain size. These are the individual slats of willow running down the length of the blade. Anything above eight grains or strips visible on the face of the bat means it's a good bat. Don't worry about knots.

And remember, no matter how well made and how expensive they are, bats break.

However, physical strength seems to be a major factor in the success of players with non-dominant bottom hands. Both Matthew Hayden and Lance Klusener are right-handers who bat left, and as many contemporary bowlers have learnt, both can hit the ball a long way. In fact, both players seem to have unusually strong bottom hands, despite these being their 'weak' hands in theory.

Hand-dominance is an essential developmental stage in children – babies who fail to pick one hand to favour over the other can develop emotional problems as they grow older. But it is possible that parents and coaches will in future begin to train both hands for co-ordination and strength, with potentially revolutionary results: a generation of ambidextrous cricketers.

BATTING TECHNIQUES

No-one will ever persuade me that there is one method of batting which can be imposed on young cricketers by the book. Let the mind of the youngster fly… show him a big field with no fielders, no barriers, no batting rules, and let him whack the ball in all directions.

Sir Vivian Richards

Many experienced coaches agree with the great West Indian's philosophy, but it is worth remembering that Sir Viv himself followed all of the basic principles of batting, even if these came to him naturally. If he had not had an instinctive grasp of the foundations of batting, he would not have been successful. For example, Richards' head was always still as the ball was delivered, which greatly aided his uncanny ability to pick the line and length early; and he also played with a very straight bat.

No matter how gifted a batsman, and how easily improvisation comes to him, the fact remains: the higher the level of cricket played, the more a batsman has to strive to be technically perfect in judging length, shot selection and shot execution.

However, before you face your first ball, there are three essential preparatory techniques that you need to create your 'ready position' or 'set up'. They are:

- **Guard** – where you stand;
- **Stance** – how you stand;
- **Grip** – how you hold your bat.

TAKING GUARD

Your guard shows you exactly where to stand as you take up your position at the wicket. More specifically, it gives you your bearings: you can't keep looking behind you to orient yourself with your off stump, and marking your guard gives you the confidence of knowing where your off stump is. This sense of where you are in the crease, and where you are in relationship to the stumps, is vital for judging line, and for deciding which balls to play and which to leave alone.

Most batsmen have been guilty of playing at too many deliveries: how often have we heard a commentator or coach saying, 'He needn't have played at that,' as a batsman trudges back to the pavilion, having been dismissed off a careless and over-expansive shot? Sir Garry Sobers simplified this idea by pointing out that if at the start of your innings, you align yourself to play only at balls that are on line with the stumps, leaving any deliveries that go wider, you are less likely to edge the ball. It seems obvious, but this ability to judge – visualizing your stumps, and knowing when they are in danger and when not – is essential in building an innings. The batsman who fails to work on developing this judgement is far more likely to play at balls he should be leaving alone, or to end up leaving balls that go on to hit the stumps.

In terms of defence therefore, it is important to understand that you only need to defend your stumps, and, when the ball bounces, your body and face. Playing away from the body – fending out or driving with the bat at arm's length – can and will lead to catches in the slip cordon. Likewise, defending square of the wicket to cover and extra cover is inadvisable: if the ball is rolling to cover, the chances are you met it outside off stump; and if it's outside off stump, and not an appropriate ball for trying to score off, what are you doing playing at it?

Which guard you choose is up to you: you know your strengths and weaknesses, and how accurately you are able to visualize where your stumps are behind you. However, whichever one you settle on, remember that your guard must allow for any pre-delivery rhythm or trigger movements, whether they be a back-and-across movement, a two-footed hop across the stumps like Brian Lara, or a quick front-on walk into line like Shivnarine Chanderpaul.

1. Leg stump

This guard is often preferred by better players, especially if they know they are strong on the off side, because it frees up the arms and allows the batsman to hit the ball from the stumps to the off side. The batsman also knows that any ball directed at his pads is now a free hit, as he is standing outside the line of leg stump and can't be out LBW.

When taking leg-stump guard, hold the bat up straight so the umpire can align its edge with leg stump, and then use the bat or your spikes to mark a line on the crease. (On scuffed and battered older pitches, it might be useful to use Chanderpaul's method of hammering a bail into the pitch, so that the position of your stump is visible as a small hole rather than a scuffmark among many other marks.) Now when

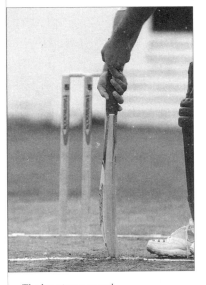

The leg-stump guard

you stand with your toes on this line or mark in a relaxed and fairly upright stance, your head will be over your leg stump.

Remember, though, that your head's position is likely to change during predelivery movements: even if you don't move around at the crease very much, you are likely to crouch, which will push your head and eyes further towards middle or off stump. Therefore, it is important to be aware of how and where your head and eyes move, so that you can stay confident about the whereabouts of your off stump. This advice holds true for all the stances.

Outswing bowlers can find it extremely difficult or frustrating bowling at batsmen who show them their stumps, which is exactly what the leg-stump guard does. If he aims at the stumps and the ball does not swing, the delivery ends up drifting into the pads, which any batsman worth his salt easily tucks away for runs. If he starts the ball on off stump, and it does swing, it allows the batsman to free his arms and hit through the off side. Also in your favour, if you choose this guard, is that if the ball swings in or moves off the seam to hit your pads, the umpire can normally see middle stump, which suggests to him that the ball was probably going on to miss leg stump. Even some doubt must go in your favour, and your innings continues.

Bob Woolmer recommended that all players learn to bat using this guard, although the final choice is a matter of personal preference. However, there are risks involved. Freeing the arms to hit a ball off middle or off stump is fine, but if that ball seams or swings late, you're going to be bowled. You also need to be a very fine judge of line and length if you're going to leave deliveries while your stumps are exposed.

The leg-stump guard is most useful when facing inswing bowlers and off-spinners on turning wickets. It can sometimes also be useful for facing reverse swing in the later overs of a match.

LEG-STUMP GUARD	
BENEFITS	**RISKS**
• Bowlers have to aim at the stumps: straight deliveries open up the leg side, and outswingers enable the batsman to free his arms with no risk of being bowled. • Umpires can be swayed by seeing your middle stump and are unlikely to give you out LBW.	• Exposed stumps can make you vulnerable to being bowled – you will need to watch line and movement carefully.

2. Middle-and-leg or 'two legs'

Taking middle-and-leg – or 'two legs' as it is also known – means that you are two inches nearer off stump. This might not seem like much, but many players feel more comfortable with the stumps behind them and their legs and body providing a kind of security blanket. Once again, the feet line up on this guard. Assuming that you have a conventional stance, the off stump should now be under your eyes.

Traditionally, there are two different ways of asking for the middle-and-leg guard – you can present either the face of the bat or its edge to the umpire.

This guard is particularly suited to players who are comfortable playing on both sides of the wicket. There are not many risks involved, although depending on how one plays, there is a possibility of being out LBW, as the body and legs are more in line with the stumps. However, this is a good guard with which to start your cricket career.

MIDDLE-AND-LEG GUARD	
BENEFITS	**RISKS**
• Off stump is in line with the batsman's eye, giving him a better sense of where off stump is. • Opens up leg-side scoring opportunities.	• Increases risk of being out LBW.

'Two legs', using the edge or face of the bat

3. Middle or centre

This guard favours batsmen who are strong off their pads, and who expect to make most of their runs on the leg side.

In this stance, your eyes will be on a line just outside off stump, making it easier to leave deliveries that start on that line. Many batsmen who take a middle-stump guard feel that they know exactly where their stumps are, while the opposite is true of bowlers: the sight of the batsman's legs and body standing squarely in front of the stumps – often hiding them entirely – tends to bother bowlers, who like to feel that they have a chance of knocking back the odd stump.

However, the risks inherent in this guard outweigh its benefits. The most obvious is the increased danger of playing around deliveries and being trapped LBW. In fact, this stance – in front of the stumps – might even provide bowlers with a target. Secondly, the batsman's eyes might be on a 'safe' line outside off stump, but that

'That's middle!'

doesn't mean he won't be tempted into playing at balls he should be leaving alone: deliveries that are well wide of off stump suddenly seem to be on a good driving line, and he can end up nicking innocuously wide balls. Finally, there is the danger of moving too far across in the crease and exposing your leg stump. We've all seen batsmen move their weight towards off stump, looking to glance or pick up the ball over mid-wicket, only to be bowled round their legs.

MIDDLE OR CENTRE GUARD	
BENEFITS	**RISKS**
• Opens up leg-side scoring opportunities. • Batsman's body and legs block the bowler's view of the stumps, which can frustrate him or upset his line.	• Increased risk of being out LBW. • Invites shots outside off stump. • Can expose leg stump.

ADVICE FOR LEFT-HANDED BATSMEN

It is always vital to know where your off stump is, but in modern cricket this is especially true for left-handed batsmen. Until recently, left-handers have enjoyed something of an advantage in cricket. This is because in order for a right-arm bowler to hit the stumps, he needs to swing the ball in (an ability in short supply in the present-day game), and most straight deliveries from a right-arm bowler aimed at the stumps must pitch outside leg-stump, leaving the batsman immune to LBW appeals. Finally, if the bowler strays onto off stump, the eventual line of the delivery gives the left-hander room to free his arms and hit the ball through the off side.

However, in the last decade or so, more bowlers have been coming around the wicket to left-handers, a method most famously and successfully used by Glenn McGrath against Brian Lara and Gary Kirsten in the late 1990s. The change in angle changes the line of off stump for the left-hander, and many southpaws find it difficult to adjust. The result is that left-handers are now as vulnerable as right-handers to being bowled, and also cannot leave the ball quite as easily as before.

Left-handed batsmen need to be even more aware of their off stump than right-handers. They also need to learn to adapt their guard and stance to cope with the challenges posed by right-arm bowlers going around the wicket. For example, it is now common for left-handers to open their stance, in other words, to stand more chest-on to the bowler. These counter-tactics used by batsmen are examined more carefully in the discussion of stances available to batters on pp. 27–34.

THE GRIP

The importance of the grip cannot be overstated: this will regulate how you swing the bat back and forwards (the biomechanics of shot-making); affect how and where you make contact with the ball; and dictate how you deal with the many variations in the bowling coming at you.

The prevalence of extremely fast short-pitched bowling in the 1970s and 80s, often aimed at the head and body, saw widespread experimentation with grips as batsmen tried to find controlled ways of keeping the ball away from their throats and faces. The advent of bouncer restrictions and the near-mandatory use of helmets at first-class levels of the game have changed this trend again, with batsmen no longer having to play high as often, and therefore not having to alter their grips too much.

But the arrival of one-day cricket presented its own challenges to traditional grips, with batsmen required to adapt and improvise their repertoire of strokes almost as a matter of course, whether working ones and twos to keep the run rate ticking over, or slogging quick boundaries.

Of course, improvisation with grips is nothing new to cricket, as evidenced by this description of the Edwardian maestro and maharajah, Ranjitsinjhi:

> When he is making a stroke his hands play up and down the handle like a violin player's on the strings of his instrument… his grip is almost entirely with finger and thumb (C.B. Fry, quoted in Synge and Anns, 1987, p. 84).

The great Ranji (as he was generally known) seems to have been as adept at improvising as any Jonty Rhodes or Michael Bevan of the twentieth century.

Being able to adapt has its place, but remember that the most important function of any grip is that it must enable the batsman to swing the bat in a straight line to hit the ball, and allow both hands to swing the bat parallel to the shoulder line. One way of checking this is to try swinging the bat like a pendulum along a straight line (preferably marked along the ground), first with the top hand, then the bottom hand, and then both together. Ensure that your feet are parallel to a line going directly down the pitch from stump to stump. If your grip is correct, the bat will follow a straight line, and both the top and bottom hand will work together. If you find that your hands force your shoulders to dip or sway, then the grip is incorrect, and an adjustment will have to be made.

It is vital that your grip feels comfortable and natural: it should enable you to hit freely all round the wicket. Once you have mastered the orthodox or basic grip, described over the page, you can make minor adjustments until you feel satisfied with the way you are hitting the ball. It is important to find out what works for you.

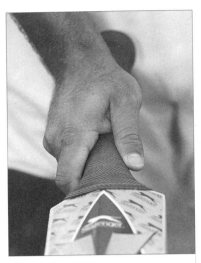

The orthodox grip – note that the handle is not being 'strangled'

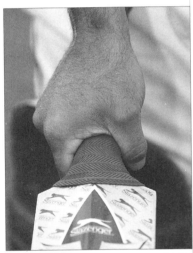

1. Orthodox grip

The natural inclination when picking up a bat is to grip it with an 'O' grip: that is, with each hand gripping the handle as one would grip the rungs of a ladder. This is often necessary when children are bought a new bat that is too heavy for them.

However, children should be taught a basic position that enables them to deal with all circumstances, and in this case the ideal grip – one that is widely taught by coaches – is the orthodox or 'V' grip.

Hold the handle with your hands not too far apart (two fingers' width is a good guideline), with the inside of the bottom arm forming a natural extension of the handle. The natural 'V' formed by the thumb and first finger of both hands should be aligned just off centre towards the outside edge of the bat. The knuckle of the forefinger of the bottom hand must point down the middle of the bat, with the knuckle above the thumb of the top hand pointing down the same line. The top hand should hold the handle firmly, while the bottom hand should be relaxed: imagine a young bird, and hold it tightly enough not to drop it, but loosely enough not to crush it.

2. The 'O' grip

The 'O' grip is very popular, perhaps because it feels more natural and more potent than the 'V' grip (this is how cavemen must have held their clubs!); but unless it is understood, it can and will cause problems, specifically when the bat is lifted or swung back.

Because of the firmness of the all-finger grip, when the bat is lifted, the elbow of the back arm slides past the bottom of the ribcage. This causes an inverted 'T' angle comprising the bottom arm and handle.

The bottom hand then slips underneath the handle, which chokes the movement of the bat and cuts down the size of the hitting area. On the downward arc, the bat starts to swing across the body, dragging the head and right shoulder down: without perfect timing, this will lead to the batsman being bowled or edging the ball into his stumps. The 'O' grip can also stifle driving opportunities on the off side through extra cover, as well as making it very difficult to play off the back foot square of the wicket.

However, it can be used with great success: some extremely prolific run-scorers (Donald Bradman, Graeme Smith and Mohammed Azharuddin, among others) have shown that if you work out where the ball can be hit safely, you can excel with an 'O' grip.

LEFT AND MIDDLE: *The choked 'O' grip forces the right elbow to move along the underside of the ribcage, with the right forearm forming an inverted 'T' with the bat handle.*

3. The Knott Grip

A further variation is the adjusted grip first used by John Edrich, and then adopted by Alan Knott in an effort to cope with the hostile fast and short bowling of Dennis Lillee and Jeff Thomson during England's 1974/75 tour of Australia. This grip helped Knott to play 'high'; in other words, to get the bat up to defend against the excessive pace and bounce that the fearsome Australian duo were generating on green and generally uneven pitches. As the grip suggests, ducking was not an option, given that the ball was rising off a length not short enough to get underneath!

This grip first evolved in front of a long mirror – the old-fashioned version of video playback. Visualizing the bounce of the ball, Knott studied the response of his hands as he adjusted the height of the bat. The first problem he encountered with the orthodox grip was that he could only reach a certain height. Therefore, he was inhibited in dealing with the ball that 'gets big' – the delivery that rises disconcertingly off the pitch, usually off an area just short of a good length on a fairly bouncy pitch, that is too full to duck beneath, but comes on too quickly to hook.

By adjusting his grip so that the top hand slipped around the back of the handle until the back of the hand was facing backwards, he found he could 'periscope' up another foot, which made the rising delivery playable. The one drawback was that the method restricted his ability to drive the ball straight: because the grip choked the free-flowing movement of the arms in the straight drive, Knott found himself push-driving for a single or two runs at best, instead of drilling the ball to the boundary rope.

However, this carefully thought-out method helped the England wicket-keeper-batsman play some fine innings during his career. Bob Woolmer counted himself among those many players who were better able to cope with ultra-quick bowling with the help of this grip.

The limiting effect the grip has on certain strokes isn't necessarily a bad thing: it certainly restricts impetuous batsmen, who might otherwise play too many adventurous shots too early on. In fact, this grip might be considered a handy means of starting to build an innings, especially against pace; once settled at the crease, you could revert to a more orthodox grip.

The bottom hand loosens and allows the full face of the bat to be offered in defence, while…

…the top hand offers a light but firm support, and is ready to lift the splice well above the batter's face.

Hingeing

A final crucial aspect of any grip is your ability to hinge, without which the backswing is impeded (try holding the bat as in the first picture – 1 – and swinging it back). This should be an automatic movement when lifting the bat behind you in your backswing. As shown in 2, the top hand should control the backward path of the bat while the bottom hand acts as a support. Children who have bats that are too heavy for them will grip the bat harder with the bottom hand, and will immediately find themselves unable to swing the bat in a straight line towards the ball.

1: *Choked grip (all the fingers are around the bat handle)*

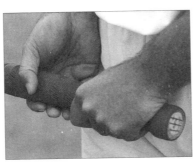

2: *Hinged grip, close-up view*

3: *Hinged grip, releasing three bottom-hand fingers to a resting position*

Summing up grips

- Players should make sure they master the orthodox grip before they begin experimenting. Hands should be in the correct position – if in doubt, check them against the illustrations above.
- The top hand should hold the handle of the bat firmly.
- The bottom hand should support the handle of the bat, rather than squeeze it: the hands and arms must be flexible and not rigid.
- Your grip must enable you to swing the bat like a pendulum along a straight line.

SOFT HANDS

No doubt you will have heard the expression 'soft hands' used to describe certain delicate shots or deft defensive strokes. In essence, this term refers to the opposite of what we have warned against in this section: 'choking' the bat, or squeezing it too hard, with disastrous effects on both your backswing and forward swing into the shot.

Hingeing is the first step in playing with soft hands: as shown in 2 and 3 opposite, rather than gripping the bat handle like a club, the bottom hand simply acts as a guide. The bottom hand quite literally holds the bat 'softly' (remember that baby bird!).

Soft hands are a defensive aid only: when hitting the ball, you will need all the force and timing that the bottom hand can provide. But when it is necessary to take the pace off the ball, soft hands are vital. By releasing the bottom hand, the impact of ball on bat is greatly diminished, which translates into the ball dropping quickly to the ground, rather than popping up to a close fielder in the case of spin bowling, or carrying to the slips off a fast bowler.

The results of not playing with soft hands are most clearly seen in beginners, who often loft easy catches to silly mid-on and mid-off because the bottom hand has forced itself past the top hand, scooping the ball into the air.

Using soft hands also means playing the ball with relaxed arms, allowing it to come on to the defensive shot, and giving with the arms as the ball arrives. Ride with the ball, don't force or punch at it. Try to relax and 'give' as the ball arrives: instead of trying to hit the ball, visualize trying to hold it on the bat for a moment before guiding it down or away.

An excellent way to develop the ability to play with soft hands is to try catching a tennis ball, thrown from three or four feet away, on a racquet without letting it bounce off. This teaches you to receive the ball with flexibility, rather than being braced or rigid.

THE STANCE

The most important consideration in choosing a stance or 'ready position' is that you must be comfortable. You must be able to move backwards or forwards quickly, easily and smoothly and you must be relaxed. Whatever stance you choose, keep your eyes level and ensure that your body weight is slightly forward of centre. (Imagine a line through your body from the head through the groin, and move your head slightly forward of that line.) This slight forward weighting will gain you vital milliseconds when the ball arrives: it is easier and therefore quicker to move back by rocking off the front foot; and the weight has already shifted to assist in the movement.

Try to 'soften' your heels – take the weight off them, but don't lift them. This should move your weight onto the balls of your feet, which in turn allows you to move forward and back when you need to. Experiment until you find out what works for you, and then practise it until you are satisfied.

1. Orthodox or sideways stance

The orthodox stance shown here is probably the best option when you first begin playing cricket. The feet should be shoulder-width apart and parallel to the batting crease. Now make sure that not only the feet, but also the knees, hips and shoulders are all parallel to the crease. Once the body is correctly lined up, roll the upper body forward, and 'sit down' slightly, so that the hands come to rest on the top of the front pad, with the bat resting on the ground.

Head, shoulder and front hip should be over the front foot, keeping the eyes level. The front elbow should point down the wicket, and the knees should be bent to allow movement forwards or backwards. It is important to keep the upper body relaxed, especially when facing quick bowlers. The position of the feet must allow the body to be in a balanced position; this enables you to move backwards and forwards with equal ease. Remember: you must feel comfortable.

It is also worth experimenting with the front foot. Sometimes by opening it up to the bowler, you will be able to move beside the ball instead of in front of it. Being beside the ball allows room for the bat to swing down the line of the ball, while if the foot goes across the line, the bat will have to swing around the front foot.

The orthodox stance: the upper body is balanced and relaxed, and the head, front shoulder, hip and knee are comfortably aligned over the front foot.

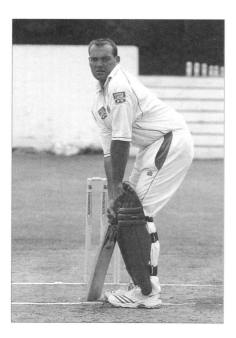
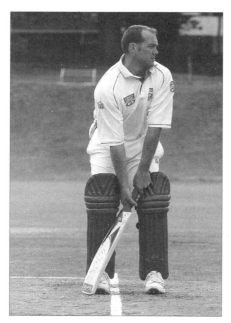

2. Wide stance

The first noticeable aspect of this stance is that the head is now slightly in front of the centre line, and in a position that is recommended by most students of the game for the reasons of weighting already discussed.

This is a stance favoured by many successful and hard-hitting batsmen. Graeme Pollock, Lance Klusener and Graeme Smith of South Africa, as well as Adam Gilchrist of Australia, have all adopted a wide stance. Not coincidentally, both Pollock and Smith are tall men, and it is a stance that seems to be particularly effective for taller batsmen, as it is less taxing on the back.

The theory behind a wide stance is that the batsman will have to move less to get to the ball, thereby eliminating movement-related errors. To play forward, you make only a sideways adjustment, and to play back, you simply rock the weight off the front foot. In effect, you've gone both forward and back before the ball is bowled, which can create enormous frustration for bowlers, and free you to score off a wider range of deliveries. If its mechanics are thoroughly understood, and it is practised diligently, this can be a very effective stance.

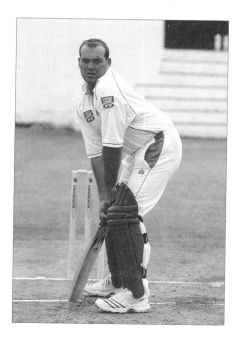

The wide stance: weight is pushed forward, player is ready to drive with minimal foot movement, or to rock back to play aggressive cross-batted shots.

Whether you stand tall with your bat off the ground (top), or take a more traditional crouch with the bat on the pitch (bottom), the open stance gives you a clearer and longer sight of the ball.

3. Open stance

The open or front-facing stance is still sometimes censured by coaches and commentators as technically unorthodox, and yet over the years it has been successfully adopted by a host of great cricketers, including Ken Barrington, Jim Parks, Peter Willey, Shivnarine Chanderpaul, Lance Klusener and Mohammed Azharuddin.

Instead of standing with his shoulders at a right angle to the wicket, the batsman opens up his front shoulder so that the line from front to back shoulder points roughly towards second or third slip.

This stance is based on the principle that standing slightly more front-on to the bowler gives the batsman a better view of the ball. The explanation for this is that just as you have a dominant hand, you also have a dominant eye, one that transmits visual signals to the brain more quickly and effectively than the other. This means that if you bat right-handed, and your right-eye is dominant, a side-on stance means that your dominant eye is having to squint away to the left over the bridge of your nose, or at least look down a line that is slightly outside that of the ball. Opening up the stance, so that there is a more direct line of sight from your right eye to the bowler's hand, can give you a better picture of the delivery. The same applies to left-eye-dominant left-handers.

A further argument for this stance is that it makes the batsman stronger on the leg side. However, in order to gain these advantages, he has to make a large movement across the stumps if he wants to drive an off-side half-volley. This extra distance he has to cover will take precious time away from his balance and shot-making processes, and may lead to a false shot outside off stump. Off-drives might not be the only shots to suffer: standing too square on can severely limit a wide variety of strokes on the off side.

There are thus advantages and disadvantages to an open stance, and you need to weigh these carefully.

4. Feet close together

If you've ever watched early film footage of cricket from the 1920s, or paged through a book of photographs of the likes of Bradman and Hobbs, you'll have seen that this used to be a very popular stance. Very few batsmen adopt this stance today, because it reduces balance; however, 70 or 80 years ago, before the advent of dangerously fast bowling and bouncy wickets, batsmen didn't need to develop as wide a range of defensive movements and shots as they do today.

It is interesting to note that those who adopted this position opened the front foot slightly and kept 60% of their weight on the back foot, ready to get forward. This was a hangover from the days of underarm bowling, when batsmen could just stay on the back foot and hammer the ball to all parts, as there was very little pace involved.

Still, before being too critical of this stance one should remember that it worked for Bradman, who faced his fair share of quick men on uneven, uncovered wickets…

© GETTY IMAGES/GALLO IMAGES

Bradman's trademark stance, with the bat face pointing at square leg and his feet almost together.

5. Closed stance

In a closed stance, the batsman's front shoulder turns towards mid-off. The line of his toes likewise points in this direction.

This stance is included here more as a warning than a recommendation: it is fraught with potential problems.

Firstly, the closed position of the body may well encourage the player to move forward and across the line of the ball, which will lead to an early foot movement known as 'planting'. This sees the batsman move outside (to the off side) of the ball, and then try to play around his 'planted' foot, usually with disastrous results if the bowler is accurate and intelligent.

Secondly – and this is more rare than players fumbling around their front foot – is the problem of batsmen allowing their back foot to slide towards the leg side. Visualize yourself stepping straight back while standing in a closed stance: you're going to head towards fine leg. In other words, you're going to expose your stumps and put yourself out of reach of off stump.

A closed stance can often be the result of poor weighting: too much weight on the front foot can turn the shoulder towards the head. This is also caused by tension and nerves, which cause the batsman to crouch too much onto the front foot. Coaches need to be on the lookout for this, and should always stress comfort and relaxation in the set-up position.

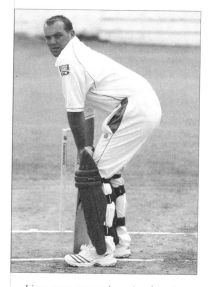

Lines gone wrong: here the player's eyes are no longer level, and to play straight, he will be forced to come around his front foot.

6. Standing tall with high backlift

This is a modern stance, pioneered by Tony Greig and then adopted with success by, among others, Mike Brearley, Graham Gooch and Clive Rice.

The stance differs from all the others discussed so far in that the batsman does not 'sit down' or crouch at the wicket, but instead stands in an upright position. Rather than resting on the ground, his bat is lifted high behind him as the ball is delivered, ready to follow through.

Those who swear by this stance say it is more restful on the back than the crouching position. In theory, the stance helps the batsman to be properly balanced, enables him to play the rising ball more easily, and stops him from toppling towards the off side, thereby preventing LBW decisions. However, this theory is flawed, as is discussed in the section on pre-delivery movements. Another potential danger is the increased vulnerability to the fast yorker: standing tall can mean that the batsman has less time to get down quickly and dig out the ball.

Summing up stances

- The orthodox stance is generally a wise place to start.
- Don't be afraid to experiment until you find the stance in which you are
  (a) most comfortable and (b) best able to play all your shots.
- Taller batsmen may find a wider or more open stance helpful.
- Whichever stance you choose, make sure it allows you to get into position quickly and easily.

Even though the player is no longer resting on his bat, he is still balanced, centred and in a good position to move forward or back.

ADAPTING YOUR STANCE TO COMBAT BOWLING TACTICS

Your guard and stance offer you security: together, they form your blueprint for successful and safe batting. However, it is the job of the bowler to erode your comfort zone and break through your defences. Intelligent or highly skilled bowlers can turn your tried and tested set-up position into a liability with just a few deliveries. When this happens, it is essential that you have the confidence and foresight to adapt in order to stay in the game. The following are some scenarios in which you might consider temporarily altering where and how you stand.

1. Leg-spin – Shane Warne ripping it out of the rough

Leg-spinners bowling over the wicket into rough is a far more common sight in cricket today than twenty years ago. To combat this tactic, stand outside leg stump – in other words, offer your exposed stumps to the bowler. Make sure to stand inside your crease, as this will cut off the angle that might allow him to bowl you around your legs. Standing outside the leg stump means you won't be tempted to play around your front pad. This also applies to a left-arm spinner.

Showing your stumps to the turning ball might seem risky, but the slightest error in line or length by the bowler means that you can free your arms and hit through the off side. In other words, the bowler is under pressure because he's turning the ball into your hitting arc. If you were standing in front of your stumps, the same delivery would force you to push out around your front leg, opening you up to all kinds of dangers, such as an LBW shout, catches to silly mid-on, or a nick to the keeper.

When you play straight to the leg-spinner turning it out of the rough, play with the spin towards the off side. But when you play across the line with a horizontal bat, always hit against the spin: if you try to pull or sweep a ball spinning in the same direction that the bat is travelling, there is a tendency to rush the wrists past the ball, whether over or under, which can result in the top-edge popping up, or the bottom edge dragging back onto the stumps, or even the back of the bat making contact with the stumps.

Most importantly, when you hit the spinning ball, hit it hard. Be committed. Don't flick after it – it's all too easy to nick off this way. In this respect, Pakistan's Mohammad Yousuf is superbly gifted: use him as a good example of how to drive with the spin. Otherwise you can't go wrong emulating V.V.S. Laxman in his stellar 2001 series against Australia in India, in which he obliterated the bowling of Shane Warne in spite of some frightening rough outside his leg stump.

2. Fast and tall – Big Bird building up a head of steam

Joel Garner, the West Indian known as Big Bird, stood at around 6 foot 8 inches tall, and it was this height that made him so difficult to play. If you tried to get into line with his bowling, you were always fending the ball from chest height; but he also bowled a brutal yorker, and if he slipped that in, you ended up playing around your legs.

The easiest way to combat this kind of attack is to stand outside leg stump, and to stand deep in the crease so that the yorker becomes a playable delivery. Anything on off stump or outside becomes a free hit or is easily left, and therefore all the pressure is switched back to the bowler.

3. Southpaw danger – Wasim Akram swinging it in from over the wicket

Bob Woolmer was being severely troubled by the left-arm inswing of Garry Sobers, until he was introduced to a useful technique by Colin Cowdrey. Cowdrey advised him to open up his stance by putting the toe of his back foot on off stump, and the toes of his front foot on leg stump. He then told him to align every shot back towards the stumps at the bowler's end – and to leave everything else. This included cutting out all shots square of the wicket. According to Cowdrey's method, the angle of delivery from Sobers would slide the ball past the face of Woolmer's bat onto the off side: playing with an open face (as Woolmer had been doing) could only lead to a snick to the slips.

In short, instead of playing the inswinger to extra cover, focus on playing it back down the wicket. All you've got to worry about then is the one that goes straight on, but because your stance is open, you'll probably miss it.

4. Keeping the slips interested – Makhaya Ntini sliding it across left-handers

This operates on exactly the same principle as above. The problem arises when left-handers see right-handed batsmen going back and across, and copy them. But going back and across only opens them out and makes them prone to nicks; or else the front foot goes across too far, and closes them off, which also leads to nicks. It is essential that left-handers keep the normal comfortable angle of their body intact, and stand still. If they move, it must be a rhythm movement that helps them to keep the angle, such as two steps forward, or to the side.

PRE-DELIVERY (TRIGGER) MOVEMENTS AND BAT-LIFT

Taking guard, finding a suitable grip, and establishing a comfortable stance are all part of your technical preparations for batting, but now that the bowler is actually on his way towards you, you need to get ready for the next step: that is, actually receiving and hitting the ball. This is where you begin to generate rhythm movements, or 'trigger' movements, as they are sometimes called – those instinctive actions you take to ready yourself and to squeeze out an extra fraction of a second before playing a shot or defending.

Many coaches will tell you that you must stand still at the crease in order to judge line and length correctly, and they are absolutely correct in principle: this is one of the keys to successful batting. But how are you supposed to stay still when the thunderbolts start crashing down at you, courtesy of Michael Holding, Waqar Younis, and others of the speedy fraternity?

The simple and frank answer is that you can't. We simply are not able to think or move quickly enough to be able to react with strength and precision once the ball has pitched. In other words, you need to develop a series of movements that take place *before* you hit the ball. Used correctly, these give you more time, and when playing fast bowlers, even a millisecond can spell the difference between an outside edge and a sweetly timed drive through the covers. Furthermore, these movements will also help you to develop that vital but often elusive asset for successful batting – rhythm.

1. Bat-lift and backswing

It seems self-explanatory that in order to hit the ball, you need to swing the bat backwards before swinging it forward; but the lifting and backward swinging of the bat are more important to your pre-delivery movements than simply as agents of leverage.

As their respective names imply, there are two movements involved in preparing to play a stroke: the reflex action of lifting the toe of the bat off the ground (bat-lift), and then the decision as to how much power you need for your shot (whether attacking or defending), which you then translate into a decision as to how far back to swing the bat (backswing).

Watch any great player and you will see this two-part action clearly, especially when they face quicker bowlers: first there is a bat-lift and then a backswing.

The bat-lift – whether a quick tap of the toe of the bat into the pitch or the feet, or a small ripple of movement through the wrist that gets the bat moving off the ground – happens simultaneously with the pre-delivery movement of the feet and body. The timing of these movements is of course entirely individual, but most batsmen share similar movements: a bend in the elbows as the bat lifts, a crouching movement and a setting of the neck, a bending and tensing of the knees. Bob Woolmer referred to this as the 'ready' position.

Ian Chappell, one of the stellar batsmen of the latter half of the twentieth century and a knowledgeable coach, describes these movements as 'unweighting'; that is, getting your weight and momentum moving in such a way as to be ready to go forward or back, depending on the delivery. Most of the great batsmen, from Donald Bradman to Jacques Kallis, developed their own methods of unweighting, according to individual preference. Interestingly, unweighting is usually only seen at the start of an innings, or against the new ball; times when the batsman needs his technique to be working at top efficiency, and when he needs to be more alert than ever. It's no

THE GREAT BACKLIFT DEBATE

Most coaches believe that if the bat does not come forward in a straight line, then the backswing must be altered until it does: countless young batsmen have been told at some stage or another that their bat is coming down from somewhere near second slip, and that they'll never be successful unless they straighten up and fly right.

It is indeed vital to bring the hands down in line with the ball, and young players should certainly be encouraged to get the fundamentals right.

But Tony Shillinglaw's challenging study of Donald Bradman's backlift has opened up a fascinating debate on the matter. This is discussed in more detail later, but Shillinglaw simply pointed out that Bradman – the most consistent run-scorer in the history of the game – brought his bat down at an angle: down from the much-maligned second slip position. Bradman was in fact far from unique in this respect: further investigation has revealed that strong batsmen such as Shahid Afridi, Adam Gilchrist and Ricky Ponting all share this trait.

The key movement, however, comes during the forward swing of the bat: a subtle but definite turn of the shoulder that straightens the path of the bat towards the line of the ball.

Straight back, or towards the slips and gully? Why not look at what today's best batters are doing? What everyone agrees on, however, is where the bat needs to end up!

coincidence that many batsmen also open their eyes very wide when unweighting, an indication of their extra alertness.

During the correct bat-lift, the front shoulder should be pointing at the ball, while the head must be absolutely still, the arms and shoulders totally relaxed, and the hands under the eyes.

The 'ready' position is crucial, as this will determine your ability to judge line and length, and it is from this position that you will decide whether or not to play at a delivery. But the backswing is as important. This is created by the shoulder turning, moving the hands into a high position, ready to hit the ball hard.

Against real pace it is vital to pick the bat up early and not too high (especially at the beginning of your innings), as this will allow you time to play the ball, as there will be less distance for the bat to travel to reach the ball.

2. Rhythm and pre-delivery movements

Batting rhythm comes from balanced, easy and minimal foot movements. Against genuine pace, these need to be made a fraction of a second before the bowler releases the ball. Against slower or medium pace bowlers there is more time, but the earlier the movement, the more time you will have to play the shot. In other words, the key to any foot movements is when (and not how) they are made.

There is a variety of movements you might like to try:

- Moving your back foot back and across towards the off stump; then transferring your weight back to the front foot as the bowler releases the ball; then making the final movement, having judged length, and playing the appropriate shot.
- Moving the front foot forwards (but not to the off side) a fraction before the bowler bowls, initiating your movements and response to the delivery as above.
- Picking up the back foot and front foot in turn and spreading them a little wider, without sideways movement, again just before the ball is released.

These are just three common ways in which rhythm is generated. Once rhythm has been achieved, these movements tend to fall away: by the time you are settled and well on your way to a century, you'll find that you are standing perfectly still, and the ball will look like a balloon.

Some players prefer to mix and combine these movements, depending on the speed of the bowling or the pace of the pitch, but as a rule of thumb, most players tend to use the back-and-across method on fast, bouncy pitches; and usually push forward on slower pitches (perhaps taking a couple of steps down the track as their unweighting movement). Once again, the longer they bat, the less they move.

Remember, it's not wise to go back and across to a spinner, since this leads to two changes of line (first your eyes, then the ball as it spins). Rather go forward or back on a straight line, especially when the ball is turning.

Chappell's definition of unweighting holds that there has to be a transference of weight from one foot to another if movement is going to be possible, in other words, you need to create momentum. Try experimenting with your own weight transference: put all your weight onto the back foot and try to move back. Not so easy! This clearly demonstrates that if you are going to move backwards, then your weight has to transfer onto the front foot and vice versa.

Every batsman will eventually develop his own unweighting movements. It is important that a player experiments until he finds a method that suits him. Coaches should also refrain from coaching only one movement or set of movements, especially their personal favourites!

The illustrations on the next page provide some practical examples of the principles and techniques described in the previous sections.

1. *Lifting the bat into a 'ready' position as the bowler approaches. This movement is used by many of today's top batsmen. From this position it is easy to defend and attack. It is important to be relaxed in this position, and to time the bat-lift together with any pre-delivery foot movements.* 2. *Note how in this front view the bat is going towards the slips. At this juncture, it is not important to lift the bat straight over the stumps; rather, aim for a relaxed lift off the ground. The arms must not tense up.* 3. *Arms relaxed, hands under the eyes, head still, watching the ball, knees bent ready to make the reflex decision.*

1. *The swing before the batsman is about to hit the ball. The shoulder turn will push the arms back and into the correct position so that the bat comes down straight. To get more power as you swing the bat back, the front wrist should 'cock' – the face of the bat will turn out towards point. Some batsmen turn the bat inwards at this moment. This is not recommended!* 2. *Going back and across just before the bowler bowls is known as a rhythm or trigger movement. This movement is used by many players to give them more time against pace, and to allow them to get in line with the stumps earlier.* 3. *The front foot press: the front foot is pressed forward and towards the off-stump. The danger here is that one can be 'trapped' and have to play around the pad.*

THE SHOTS

If you want to write a novel, you need a good vocabulary and a firm grasp of grammar. A Test match innings is a cricketer's novel, created slowly and carefully for his own pleasure and that of his teammates and supporters; and in this instance, shots are his grammar and vocabulary. Without a cricketing vocabulary, you simply can't craft an innings: like many people who are not good writers, you might have a splendid idea (a match-saving defensive innings, a match-winning century), but without the nuts-and-bolts grammar, you won't know where to start.

What follows is an explanation of every possible batting shot – the full repertoire. Whether you should play them all is another matter entirely. Too many batsmen fail because they play all the shots all the time. Just as a novelist adapts and restricts his or her language according to the subject matter and reader, so the batsman must discipline himself and learn which shots are appropriate to which conditions and circumstances.

How many shots should you have? The simple answer is: all of them. Some Test batsmen have managed at international level with an apparently limited range of strokes – South Africa's Kepler Wessels (who played for Australia as well) is a case in point, as is Steve Waugh, who slowly but surely *eliminated* shots from his repertoire during his long and distinguished career – but even such players have enough shots to get by. Younger batsmen can sometimes feel pressured into learning and playing strokes that don't suite their game or temperament, just as others can become lazy or inhibited, afraid of extending their options and relying instead on the small range of strokes they know and trust. If you are uncertain of where you stand, memorize this basic yardstick: if you can score on both sides of the wicket, stop getting yourself out, and manage not to get bogged down against spin – then you have enough shots.

Of course, there are some shots that you must have, especially at higher levels. During England's tour of South Africa in 2005, Kevin Pietersen dealt destruction and mayhem to the home-team's bowlers in the one-day series; yet at no stage was his inability to cut tested. This weakness was successfully exploited by Warwickshire earlier in his first-class career: they simply put on a left-arm seamer who bowled short and wide outside Pietersen's off stump, and he holed out to gully every time, rarely reaching double figures. He has since worked on that aspect of his game and gone on to be a phenomenal shot-maker at international level, but for a time, it was a huge gap in his armoury, and effectively made him irrelevant as a front-line batsman.

Training and practice are everything in shot selection. By learning the shots, learning (as Peter May put it) the correct answer to every question asked of you, and practising them over and over again, you will be able to react effectively and powerfully when the time comes.

STRAIGHT BAT SHOTS

Many traditional coaching methods have been overtaken and outdated by the rapid development of the game in recent decades, but it's unlikely that coaches will stop telling batsmen to play straight anytime soon. Playing straight, with a vertical bat, both defensively and when attacking, is the essence of batting. All the masters of the game have played straight, which is all the evidence you should need to encourage you to learn and master the straight bat shots.

Playing straight also makes mathematical sense: on the face of an upright bat there is six times the area in which the ball can make contact than there is on the bat that is held horizontally. In other words, it is considerably easier to hit the ball with a straight bat.

One of the most commonly seen dismissals is caused by playing across the line of the ball with the bat at an angle, usually resulting in a catch in the slips or the ball being dragged onto the stumps. Right-handed left-handers – batsmen who bat left-handed but who are right-handed – are more susceptible to playing with an angled bat, because their bottom hand does not have the strength or co-ordination necessary to swing the bat straighter. As discussed in the section on grips (pp. 23–26), it is up to the bottom hand to adapt its grip if the bat is going to be allowed to straighten.

Experiment with your own bat by wrapping more and more fingers around the handle: you will notice how the bat's angle changes as you add more fingers to the grip. Players with weaker bottom hands will inevitably want to have more fingers on the handle for comfort, which tends to cost them in the long run.

It's been stated here before, but it's worth repeating: training the bottom hand is a vital part of coaching the art of batting. It's been dormant for 90 years, and that's 90 years too long!

1. THE FORWARD DEFENSIVE

One often hears that teaching the forward defensive shot to young cricketers can dampen their enthusiasm for the game. We disagree. In fact, teaching young players cricket shots without first ensuring that they master this one is tantamount to teaching them to ski or roller-blade without first showing them how to stop.

We would be the last to discourage a young player from hitting the ball – after all, the nature of the game demands that runs be scored. However, if bowlers consistently bowl a good length, then batsmen will have no choice but to meet their deliveries with appropriate shots. This being the case, the argument for learning the forward defensive is very strong. Without this skill very few innings would last very long, a sure-fire way of killing a young player's interest in and enjoyment of the game.

Statistics show that during an average innings of 100 (if such an innings can ever be called average), the forward defensive shot comprises nearly 70% of all shots offered during that innings. This was well illustrated by Jacques Kallis's anchor innings of 95 against India in Bangalore in February 2000, which enabled South Africa to win by an innings and 71 runs. Kallis faced a gruelling 359 balls, almost twice as many as faced by the next-highest scoring batsman. He later remarked that halfway through the innings, he thought he was too tired to play one more forward defensive stroke, underlining that this stroke is the foundation on which most innings are built.

The forward defensive is just that: the first line of defence for your stumps. And just because it is a basic and unglamorous stroke, don't assume it is easy. In essence, you are defending a target that is 9 inches (22,86cm) by 28 inches (71,1cm), from a missile the size of a jaffa orange (hence the exclamation, 'That ball was an absolute Jaffa!'), with a bat that is 36 inches long, 4 inches wide and weighs at least two and a half pounds. In theory, it's easy, but in real life, it is much harder than one expects.

When to play the shot

The forward defensive is played to a ball that cannot be driven, and that is too full to go back to. It is played when the bowler is attacking the stumps, as opposed to bowling in the tricky line just outside off stump. In other words, it is played to a threatening delivery on a good line and length. Remember that a good length ball will differ according to the height – and therefore the reach – of the batsman, the pace and bounce of the pitch, and often the position of the game (for instance, two identical deliveries can look dramatically different if the first arrives with your team on 450 for 3, and the second arrives in the final session as you try to hang on for a draw). A rough guide for what constitutes a good length ball is usually something around three metres from the batting crease.

There is an old saying: 'If in doubt, push out.' This is based on the assumption that the umpire will not give you out on the front foot, so the further forward you go, the more likely you are to be given the benefit of the doubt in case of LBW appeals. With the advent of technology, which has made umpires less inclined to give batsmen the benefit of the doubt, this adage has become a little ragged, and there have been some shocked batsmen walking back to the pavilion, who felt certain they were practically doing the splits when the ball hit their front pad!

However, if the ball is moving around a lot off the seam or keeping low, it is better to try and meet it early to prevent movement, just as a goal-keeper in football might narrow the angle to make the shot harder. Hence the advice to 'get to the pitch of the ball to smother the spin.' If you're at the pitch of the ball and it deviates, it can only deviate into the middle of your bat, or at most an inch either side of the middle.

Playing the shot

Watch the ball out of the bowler's hand, and pick line and length as soon as possible, with the head kept absolutely still (1). Take a comfortable stride towards, and just inside, the line of the ball; keep the eyes level, swing the bat back and over the stumps by making a small front shoulder rotation. Cock the wrist of the top hand and release the fingers of the bottom hand, holding only with thumb and first finger (2). At this moment, the face of the bat should be slightly open and the backswing should take the top hand back past the knee. The front hip should be balanced over the front foot, and head and shoulder should be together (3).

At the moment of impact, the heel of the back foot is raised to allow the batsman's weight to get forward: don't leave the heel on the ground, as this causes poor balance. Rotate the front shoulder towards the ball, and allow enough room with your front foot to enable the path of the bat to meet the path of the ball. It is important to remain sideways on, and to bring the bat down straight and square to the line of the ball, travelling parallel to the initial position of the shoulders, past the back pad (so that the ball cannot nip through) to join the front pad. The bottom of the bat and pad must be kept together, with the hands high over the ball. The body should be balanced, with the hip over the front foot and only the toe of the back foot resting on the ground for stability (4 and 5).

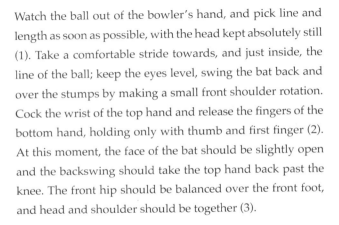

As you play the stroke, the top hand should be dominant, remaining in front of the bottom hand (this will angle the bat and keep the ball down), while the bottom hand releases the full grip so that only the thumb and forefinger remain to guide the bat into position.

Meanwhile, keep the top elbow high, the head and eyes over the ball, and the eyes on the ball (for as long as is possible), which at this point should be bouncing onto the bat and then rolling harmlessly away.

Remember, don't make any effort to force the ball away: you should feel that your bat is an impenetrable, immobile wall rather than a blade.

Practising the shot

A mirror is an excellent tool for practising the various phases of the forward defensive: watch every part of yourself as you make the shot – feet, shoulders, elbows and hands. Then practise in degrees of progression, first with a partner throwing underarm with a tennis ball; then throwing a cricket ball underarm; then overarm bowling with a cricket ball; and then finally a bowling machine. If you don't have access to a bowling machine, get your partner to throw (or bowl, if he is consistent enough) at the correct length. If you make a mistake judging length, try to stay in position and survive.

Whether you use a mirror or video footage to examine your technique, it is important to try to 'feel' the correct positions, to train your body to assume the correct positions until they become second nature. Make sure that you start at a slow, manageable pace so that the accent is on the correct body shape. As you become better at the shot, gradually increase the pace of the ball until finally reaching competitive levels. Also remember to practise the shot against spin and seam wherever possible.

Common problems

- **The extra-cover defensive:** a common error, in which the batsman pushes out towards extra cover with an angled bat. This technique presents only half a bat to the line of the ball, and any movement off the pitch or through the air will either find an edge, nip between bat and pad and bowl you 'through the gate', or miss the bat altogether, which can be psychologically disconcerting, and will certainly unleash a torrent of commentary from the opposition!
- **Hard hands:** pushing hard at the ball while defending. This can create a variety of problems, the most dangerous of which is that if the ball hits the edge, it will carry comfortably to the slips. Likewise against spin, the hard push will give the ball the impetus to fly neatly into the hands of the fielders around the bat. Even

if you evade these dangers, the ball will still travel too quickly to the infield to enable a single to be stolen. Finally, if you push out past the front pad, a gap (the infamous 'gate') will appear, and any inward movement by the ball will take it through and into your stumps. This is especially true on slow pitches where the ball 'holds up' on the surface. In other words, don't confuse the forward defensive with the defensive push, which is a legitimate shot used when the batsman is trying to push the ball into a gap for a single or to steer the ball off the back foot down to third man. However, even this shot, a product of one-day cricket, is fraught with danger and it is often punished by dismissal. In fact if you're going through a lean trot or a run of bad form, don't even think about playing it.

- **Defending across the line:** bringing the bat down across the line is a common fault and needs to be eradicated early on. What looks like a good forward defensive ends up with the bat carrying on across the pad, with the result that the batter is either bowled (off the outside edge or simply past the outside edge), or caught behind off the outside edge.

- **Bent back knee:** to get forward and over the ball properly, your back knee needs to be fairly rigid, with your back leg stretched out behind you, toes on the ground and heel in the air. When the back knee is bent, the entire shot becomes more upright, leading to serious trouble.

  The cause of this error is an incorrect body position: the body is out of control, largely because there is no balance being provided by the back knee, which means there is no guarantee that if the ball moves, the body will be able to respond. Most obviously, the bat is stuck behind the front knee and can't go any further if the ball turns or seams in towards the pad, which will almost certainly end in an LBW dismissal.

Geoffrey Boycott, one of the most dogged defenders of a cricket ball in history, was very clear on how to play the forward defensive: 'Do not push out in hope. Do not be in doubt. Make up your mind. Be positive.' As Boycott knew, being positive doesn't necessarily mean going hard at the ball with bat, body and hands. It means that the decision to defend can be a positive one.

TO PAD OR NOT TO PAD?

Pad play – the tactic of pushing the ball away with the pads, pretending to play, but keeping the bat well clear of actual contact with the ball – is often used in conjunction with the forward defensive. It can be an important defensive strategy on turning pitches in the subcontinent, and was also a major factor in English cricket for years, on the uncovered pitches once called 'sticky dogs'.

Pad play is still very much in vogue against spinners, as it is very difficult for an umpire to give the batsman out LBW if the ball is turning prodigiously: on a turning pitch, with the ball pitching outside off and spinning in, it can be a life-saver. To pull it off correctly, you need to make sure that the ball is covered by your pad, with your bat tucked in behind it, so that to the umpire it looks as if you're about to play it. When it does turn, you subtly shove the ball with the front pad and then finish by playing a forward defensive shot well after the ball has gone, hopefully with enough panache and determination to deceive the umpire into thinking you've played a bona fide shot! Be warned, however, that pad play is not readily tolerated by modern umpires, and often makes them more inclined to favour bowlers' LBW appeals.

On pitches where the ball is moving around a great deal, whether through seam or spin, it is more advisable to look to play the ball, only taking the bat out of the way at the last minute if the delivery does too much. This way, if the ball goes straight on, you can play it comfortably.

Colin Cowdrey's advice to a young Bob Woolmer was clear: always make an effort to hit the ball, and leave it at the last minute if necessary. He called this method 'playing to leave', and found it preferable to leaving the ball and then trying to adjust to hit it at the last moment.

2. BACKWARD DEFENSIVE AND BACK GLANCE

When a boy at Rugby, 'Plum' [Warner] first heard the down-to-earth maxims… most apposite for the leg glance: 'Lean on her, Sir' and 'Smell her, Sir, smell her'. Together, these phrases might better advise the budding batsman how to play the stroke than the many words, diagrams and photographs that have been published in the coaching books over the last fifty years (Synge and Anns, 1987, p. 85).

Aggressive fast bowling reached a peak in the late 1970s as the pace attacks mounted by the West Indian and Australian bowlers put batsmen through the mill, the likes of Michael Holding, Joel Garner, Dennis Lillee and Jeff Thomson taking the game by the scruff of the neck and shaking it. Severe injuries were common, and tensions often flared, with accusations of bullying bandied around. The introduction of batsman-friendly laws and rapid improvements in the quality of helmets and other protective gear has meant that the fast bowling threat has been reduced in the modern game. Nevertheless, the short, rising delivery is still very much in vogue today.

This is why it is essential for every batter to master the backward defensive, to cope with deliveries that bounce steeply off a good length. Indeed, many aspiring young cricketers have been found wanting at the higher levels of the game because of their inability to cope with the rising ball. Schoolboys must learn to play off the back foot, as during their formative years they will have mostly played forward, due to the innocuous pace of the bowlers they will have faced, and the low, slow pitches they will have played on. Schoolboy bowlers lack the strength and height to generate pace and bounce, and as a result young batters never have to face balls bouncing dangerously at their chests and throats, and can play forward most of the time.

These factors conspire to leave batsmen one-dimensional, lacking the variety of shots necessary to become exceptional players. At the highest levels of the game, any inability to play a particular shot will be ruthlessly exploited by bowlers able to land the ball precisely where they wish. This is why it is essential to learn and become proficient in all the possible cricketing strokes from a young age.

When to play the shot

Backward defensive: while the forward defensive shot protects the stumps, the backward defensive is mainly used to defend the body against balls pitching short of a good length and bouncing to waist height and above.

Back glance: this is played to a shorter ball that rises or cuts back towards the front hip, stomach or groin. Younger and more inexperienced players often jump away to the leg side instinctively when the ball cuts back into their mid-section, instead of playing it off their hip. This evasive action often results from having been hit a painful blow in the past, which is why it is so important that youngsters wear thigh-pads, a box, and ideally a chest pad as well.

Short-pitched bowling tests the courage of all players. Backing away is the first sign of fear, unless it is done for a specific reason (making room to play an attacking shot, usually in one-day cricket). As soon as the batsman displays fear, the bowler will smell a wicket, knowing that he has unnerved the batsman. Apart from renewing the energy and focus of the bowling, the batsman who backs away exposes his stumps and opens himself up to a wide variety of dismissals: being bowled, edging the ball into the stumps, being caught in the slips or gully, and so on.

Being able to get into line is an important skill to have in the multi-day game. It takes courage, but it also sends a strong message both to your teammates and to the opposition: Ian Redpath and Brian Close were two international players who were particularly admired for being willing to take the ball on the body without flinching.

Playing the shot: backward defensive

The initial movement of the backward defensive, as shown in the second frame, is for the back foot to go back and across towards the off stump, with the head behind the line of the ball and the shoulder pointing at the trajectory of the delivery. Be careful not to get your head outside the line of off stump: there's no point risking an edge defending an area that isn't threatening either your stumps or your body.

The third frame shows how the front foot then slides back and rests on its toe next to and just behind the heel of the back foot. This will help you balance, since all the weight will now be on the back foot. Initially, the front shoulder should be pointing at the line of the ball. The bat should swing through in a straight line towards the ball's trajectory. (The path of the bat comes from just inside the line of the right shoulder.)

Coaches teaching the backward defensive must make it clear that the ball will be bouncing above waist height, and that defending the body will be more important than defending the stumps. Therefore it is crucial that young batsmen are also taught how to leave the ball off the back foot as part the learning progression of this shot.

Alan Knott's 'periscope' grip (right) is described in the section on grips (see p. 25), and his method might be worth practising along with the conventional backward defence. Release three fingers of the top hand, holding the bat with thumb and first finger. This allows the bat to be raised higher to cope with the excessive bounce.

Few school players will be facing balls that get that high, but in more competitive cricket, some of the quick men can get the ball up frighteningly high and fast. Facing bowlers like Michael Holding, Bob Woolmer found he had almost no time to deal with the ball: playing a normal defensive shot could mean the ball hitting and breaking his forearm. The grip shown here helped him lift the bat above shoulder level so the handle was above his eye line, enabling him to keep the ball down. A rather grim advantage is that this exposes the fleshy part of the arm, which is less susceptible to a fracture.

YOU'RE SO SQUARE!

No coach or commentator can mention the backward defensive without immediately drawing fire in a debate that has raged for decades: whether or not the shot should be played sideways or square on.

The reality is that both methods can be successful, and both methods can be disastrous. In the end, perhaps it's wisest not to be dogmatic about which is better; instead, allow the height of the bouncing ball to dictate the best way to play the shot.

For example, if the ball is bouncing controllably and you're looking to attack, then sideways is the better option, as this allows the bat to swing through the correct path. If the body is in the way (square on), then the bat will come down from the direction of gully and swing out in a 'U' shape towards the ball. Thus contact will be limited, and you're more likely to get an edge than to score. But if the ball nips back, it becomes tricky to play sideways on, as the body is in the way of the bat.

There is no final answer: Ken Barrington, the famous defensive England batsman, preferred the square-on method, as did Sir Donald Bradman; Ted Dexter preferred the sideways method. Let's agree to disagree!

Playing the shot: back glance

The first movements of the back glance are essentially those of the backward defensive: a step back and across to get into line with the off stump (1 and 2). However, if the ball nips back towards your body, it is time to turn the defensive shot into a run-scoring one.

Turn the body square on, and move the bat across your body into the line of the ball. Stop when that line has been reached – in other words, have the bat waiting for the ball to arrive, rather than pushing out at the ball (3).

If possible, don't go further outside your body than your front pad: it is just as dangerous to play outside your body on the leg side as it is on the off, and few dismissals are as frustrating as being strangled down the leg side.

The hands then rotate down with a firm twist of the wrists, deflecting the ball down to fine leg (4 and 5): at this point the bottom hand should be holding the bat only with thumb and forefinger. As the ball makes contact, the bat is slightly angled, and as the shot is completed, the left foot goes backwards, allowing you to turn completely. The hands remain over the ball with the top hand in front of the bottom one. The bat has now turned, and the ball has run away to fine leg, allowing you to trot through for a single, or, if the contact was finer and the ball speedy, adding another four runs to your total.

If you are going to play the back glance safely and effectively, there are two golden rules to remember:

- **Keep your eyes glued to the ball throughout** (don't flinch or blink as the ball rises up towards your face).
- **Never play across the line.**

Like all the shots, the backward glance can become a reflex if practised enough.

Practising the shots

Start by practising the movements in front of a mirror to ensure that everything is correct and moving as it should be. Next, ask a partner to throw a tennis ball from a distance similar to where the ball might pitch; that is, up at your body from a point low to the ground short of a good length (1). Focus particularly on stopping the ball and allowing it to land at your feet. When you are confident that the shot is working, move on to using a cricket ball, first thrown up at you, and then bounced at you at pace (2).

Once the backward defensive is well on the way to becoming grooved, start combining it with the back glance. Be warned: this will not be easy, and the movement of the leg glance will take some co-ordinating, but practice and patience will help to eliminate the fear factor. Remember to use a thigh pad and good pair of gloves: coaches don't always have the most accurate throwing arms!

Mastering the backward defensive and the back glance will remove the temptation to back away to leg. In addition, like the glance off the front foot (to be discussed shortly), the back glance is extremely useful for picking up steady singles.

An interesting development of the back glance is found on the Asian subcontinent. Players from India and Pakistan are traditionally extremely wristy (meaning that their wrists are very strong and yet highly flexible, allowing them to work the ball into angles more forceful players struggle to pick out). Since the back glance employs the wrists, and Asian pitches tend to be less bouncy, players in this region find it far easier to connect well with back glances. In India and Pakistan, the shot has transformed into something of a leg clip that goes behind square leg, providing rich pickings in terms of boundaries.

1. *Flicking the ball up off the pitch at the body to simulate a rising delivery.*
2. *Bouncing the cricket ball at the body, a more typical 'throw-down'. (Note that Kallis is lifting his bat in the direction of the slips, not directly backwards.)*

However, if mistimed, it can easily bring about a dismissal, since the ball remains in the air for much longer than it does after a conventional glance. This Asian variation has in fact given rise to a new fielding position, a slightly deeper forward short-leg specifically designed to catch that clip shot.

Common problems with the backward defensive

- **Defending towards cover:** we have already highlighted the dangers of playing a forward defensive towards extra-cover, and a similar flaw often creeps into the execution of the backward defensive: a tendency to play back defensively to balls rising well outside the off stump, and to push out towards the off side. The danger here is similar to that of the extra-cover forward defensive, as any away movement will mean an edge to the slips.

  This is a common fault, and one caused mostly by coaches remaining adamant that the batsman should be sideways-on when defending. They are right in insisting that the first movements should ensure that the body is in a side-on position, but they should accept that the final defensive shot is played front-on; in other words, in a square position.

- **Grip too tight:** holding the bat too tightly with the bottom hand will almost always lead to an awkward body movement – the head will bend to the right, forcing the eyes outside the line of the ball. Furthermore, if the ball hits the hands at any pace, and the fingers are clenched and unable to move quickly, broken bones can result, with the dreaded result of a six-week absence from the game.

FRONT-FOOT DRIVES

Of all the pleasures cricket provides, and in all the satisfaction gained from playing shots correctly, few things match the thrill of drilling a straight cover or on drive through the field to the boundary. For batsmen, driving is as good as it gets.

When to play these shots

All the shots listed here are played to a half-volley or a low full toss. They can also be played on the up, which means hitting the ball as it rises off a good length. However, hitting on the up should be informed by the state of the pitch: you need to be confident of the ball's bounce and carry before you start playing cavalier shots on the up.

1. OFF DRIVE, STRAIGHT DRIVE

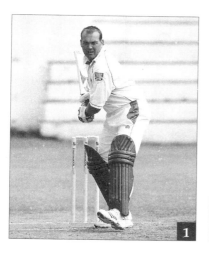 

Take a balanced step forward towards the bowler (1), with the weight on the front leg and the heel of the back foot raised, so that you can place your front foot beside the pitch of the ball. The back foot should roll onto the toe, and not swivel; if the back toe swivels, it causes the body to square up, which will hinder the execution of the shot and make the hands work across the body, leading to a nick to the slips.

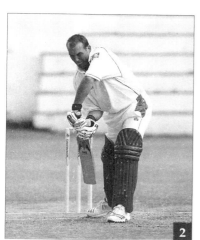 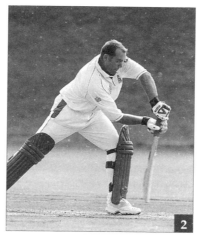

Swing the bat down in an imaginary line from the toe of your back foot to the pitch of the ball. Make contact under your eyes (as in 2), making sure the wrist of the top hand is in front of the bottom hand (2 on the right) if you want the ball to go along the ground.

Depending on your swing and the momentum of the shot, you can use the check-drive follow-through, favoured by batsmen such as Colin Cowdrey, Jacques Kallis and Sachin Tendulkar.

   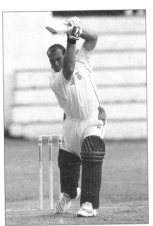

The front elbow pivots up high, and the bat is stopped in its swing before rotating up past the horizontal and over the shoulder (as shown above). As we will learn later, the value of the follow-through is largely diagnostic; it indicates that the batsman has played the shot fluently and correctly, maintaining good balance throughout. It reminds the batsman (and the bowler!) that the batsman is in control of his shots.

An alternative to this approach is the follow-through drive, named thus as the drive is allowed to 'flow' naturally through its entire motion without being checked. At the top of the drive the wrists 'break' (5 below), causing the hands to turn inwards towards the leg side.

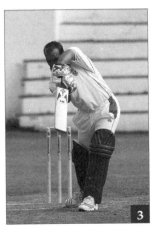   

Frames 3 and 4 show the final position of the follow-through drive: the wrists have rolled over and through, and the bat handle is now facing where the ball has gone. This is a very complex wrist movement, sometimes referred to as 'wringing the dishcloth' because of the twist of the wrists required. Unless this is practised regularly and perfected, it can lead to problems: a common fault is to turn the wrists too early in the shot and therefore end up mistiming the ball, getting an inside edge as the bat face starts to come across the line of the delivery.

This method was favoured by greats such as Bradman and Hutton, and in the modern era, Rahul Dravid (among others) demonstrates this follow-through with great panache.

2. COVER DRIVE

All drives come from the same base: they differ only in where you want the ball to go. The cover drive is played later than the straight drive and the on drive. Allow the ball to come past the front foot, turn the front shoulder to the area you wish to place the ball, and then ensure that the hands work on the same line, hitting and guiding the ball through the cover region.

Be wary of driving square of the pitch too early in your innings: misjudging the length of a delivery can bring the slips and gully into the game, and send you out of it. Remember that when using an angled bat, you are using only half a bat – sometimes even less – when playing through the covers. Timing and balance have to be perfect if this shot is to be successful: inefficient balance and technique – or undisciplined hands – can all too often lead to a slip catch.

Poorly co-ordinated hands will also cost you dearly on slow pitches: the hands rushing past the ball will often bring an inside edge down onto the delivery, and in turn onto your stumps.

The full flow of the cover drive. The angle here is deceptive: the batter has played the ball almost under his eyes.

3. ON DRIVE

The on drive is one of the more difficult front-foot strokes, played to a delivery pitched up on middle- or leg stump: many batsmen prefer not to commit to an attacking stroke with their wickets under threat, and opt for a defensive push instead. Indeed, very few international batsmen have made this their trademark shot, although Sachin Tendulkar is particularly strong straight down the ground between the bowler and mid-on, an indication of his superb ability to judge length, and his perfect balance at the crease.

Make sure that your shoulder points towards the ball, then move your front foot just outside the line of the ball, i.e., towards the on side (1 and 2). Make contact under or just in front of your eyes: the on drive is played fractionally earlier than the cover drive, and you need to time it perfectly so that you are not reaching for the ball, but also not too late on it, killing it into the pitch at your feet (3). Don't play across the line of the ball: try to hit it back past the bowler on the on side, rather than working it square through mid-wicket (4 and 5).

DRIVING ON THE UP

Hitting the ball a few milliseconds after it has pitched and bounced is risky, but to the well-set batsman on a good pitch it can pay excellent dividends, as well as having a dramatically demoralizing effect on the bowler and his captain. Most drives can be played on the up, but for the purposes of this discussion, we will examine two: the on drive and the check drive.

The on drive played on the up requires extreme skill, an even-paced surface and excellent timing. Make sure that you play the shot towards mid-on: the ball may well squirt off the bat and go square of the wicket, but the bat path must remain in the well-documented 'V' between mid-on and mid-off.

The shot begins with both feet brought together on or about leg stump: this will allow the ball slightly more room to come at you. The bat is swung normally, but instead of timing the stroke to meet the ball under the eyes, the shot is 'early', so early in fact that the ball is struck about two feet in front of the eyes. This requires fantastic hand-eye co-ordination, and if properly executed, oozes class. However, beware if the ball swings late: movement after the shot has begun can easily result in edges, or missing the ball completely, and the resulting ignominy of being clean bowled.

If you're trying to perform this stroke and failing, don't despair: it requires immense skill and timing, and conditions also have to be perfect if you're to play it with absolute confidence.

The second drive that is hit 'on the up' is the push or check drive. This is normally played to a good length ball (as opposed to a half-volley) where more control is needed; in other words where the ball isn't squatting down on a full length and begging to be hit. It is a shot best restricted to a good surface with true bounce.

Basically it is a stiff-armed push, which comes with its own dangers: if the ball 'stops' on the surface (slows dramatically), it is almost impossible to stop your swing, with the result that the ball is played far too early, and usually loops up to a grateful cover or mid-off fielder.

So why play the check drive at all? The answer lies in its history. Because pre-Second World War batsmen had a tendency to roll the wrists early in the follow-through drives, coaches – and many players – set about developing a drive that would keep the face of the bat on line with the ball for longer. This, together with the advent of heavier bats, which gave more value for less impact, resulted in the modern check drive.

In other words, it is a modern version of the traditional drive, which was developed in the 1950s to overcome the problems sometimes experienced in executing the more flamboyant and complicated drives preferred by the likes of Don Bradman, Jack Hobbs, Len Hutton and Wally Hammond. Nonetheless, the classic wristy drive played properly has a larger impact area, cutting down the risk of late movement. The push drive is extremely vulnerable to late movement of the ball.

Therefore, like any shot, it has to be practised a great deal. The push drive is more often used in one-day cricket to nudge the ball into gaps, and it is worth remembering that looking to score, especially by playing on the up, will always be more dangerous than putting away a true half-volley.

Having said that, it is worrying to note that the check drive has increasingly crept into the four-day game, where it often leads to soft dismissals: we see players caught in the covers and at gully, as batsmen become vulnerable to a well-bowled slower ball. Instead of trying out this shot on a tricky track during a cat-and-mouse four-day game, rather wait until conditions are perfect – a good pitch with no seam movement, a soft ball, and spread field – before trying it out.

Practising the shots

The most effective way to practise all the variations of the front-foot drive is to use progressive training. This is a system that gradually builds skills upon skills in a manner that makes sense both in terms of the batsman's thought processes and his biomechanics, until finally the complete shot has become a reflex action. When the batsman recognizes a specific delivery, his progressive training will mean he is fully equipped to know how, when and why to play the shot he has selected.

The following general routine can be applied to almost all the drives described above.

- **Start with a stationary ball placed on an upside-down paper cup** (there should be a small rim on the base of the cup to prevent the ball from rolling off).
- **Practise the mechanics of the shot by placing your feet in the correct position,** and then hit the ball, allowing the arms to work.
- **Move back into your stance position.** Now move your feet into the correct position and hit the ball. (Coaches can also set up targets for batsmen to hit, such as gaps between cones, if these are required.)
- **Get your coach or partner to roll a ball towards you,** and put your foot alongside the ball and hit it through the target area or back to the roller.
- **Introduce timing:** get your partner to stand next to you on the off side (leg side if you're practising the on drive), and have him drop a tennis ball on a driving length. Move your foot alongside the pitch, but hit it only on the second bounce, as illustrated in this sequence.

- **Now progress to underarm throws:** get your partner to throw from about three metres in front of you, and hit to both the off side and the on side (so as not to kill the thrower!).

- **Send him back to throw from about 15 metres away, overarm.** It's very important that he throws accurately; if necessary, threaten him with a few straight drives to get him focused!

- **Progress to a bowling machine, working on each length for a period of time** – bowling machines groove shots, and shouldn't be used to simulate random deliveries on random lengths.
- **Finally move into a conventional net with standard net bowlers.**

One of the most fundamental processes you can discover in progressive training is how transferring your weight increases power in the shot, and how best to execute this transfer. The easiest and best way to experiment with this is to practice what Bob Woolmer called one-foot driving. The idea is not to stand on one foot and try driving, but rather to hit the ball and then lift up the back foot a split second later. This will allow you to feel the effect of the weight transference.

Move into position as you normally would, and play the drive (1 and 2). As you make contact, lift your back foot off the ground: as illustrated, you should be able to balance on your front foot (3, 4 and 5). If you fall forward from this position, you will know that your weight is not properly transferred – your shots will be suffering as a result.

A common problem: turning inside-out

This can happen when you try driving at a ball in front of you. Reaching for the ball has the effect of turning the body to a more square-on position in the crease, with the front shoulder facing square leg and the back shoulder aiming at cover point. Once the shoulders move, the hips follow. Suddenly your bat is forced to come down from gully along the line of your body, and then somehow move out again towards the off side.

This is known as batting 'in to out' or 'inside out', and instead of swinging through the line, you will find yourself slicing the ball. Obviously, this position can be useful when playing the ball square on the leg side, but if you are driving the ball on or just outside your off stump, the poor swing of your bat will cause severe problems. The solution is simple, however: play alongside the ball, and play along parallel lines as explained before.

CROSSED LINES: HITTING STRAIGHT AND ACROSS THE LINE

Coaches spend a great deal of time telling batsmen to 'hit straight' and to 'play through the line', but Bob Woolmer (who owned up to being one of these coaches) knew that an eleven-year-old, a fifteen-year-old and a Test player will all present different interpretations of what those instructions mean. So what exactly are we talking about when we encourage batters to play through the line of the ball?

When the ball leaves the bowler's hand, its trajectory creates a line in your mind's eye that points to where it will pitch. Any movement will change the line slightly, but in general it continues through to the wicket-keeper, unless there is some intervention by the batsman, who will intercept that invisible line with the invisible line of his own swing.

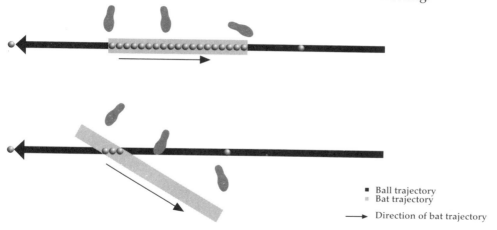

■ Ball trajectory
■ Bat trajectory

→ Direction of bat trajectory

FIGURE 2: *The lines followed by bat and ball*

In order to play a shot correctly, the bat line must meet the ball at the contact or crossing point (see the top line in Figure 2) but must remain on that line to execute the shot. The challenge that arises when playing across the line is that the hitting area becomes much smaller (the bottom line in Figure 2). More skill and timing is required to play sideways, which is why bowlers strive for lateral movement. This also explains why the measure of a skilled and world-class batsman can be judged by whether he has mastered the ability to play across the line.

Hitting a cover drive means that the hands and bat must follow through on the shoulder and feet line; this is vital if they are to make contact. Any change to the swing will almost certainly result in failure to make contact – or an edge.

Summing up the drives

- When driving on the front foot, make sure that the weight is transferred forward, through the hip and knees into the foot.
- As a general rule when driving, keep the back foot still with the heel lifted. Use it as the fixed point in the shot, while moving the front foot around in a half-circle. This will enable you to drive in an arc from point to mid-wicket.
- Get your foot down the wicket towards and beside the pitch of the ball, with your toes pointing at the ball.
- Leave yourself enough room to swing the bat.
- When you pick up your hands and move them back into the backswing, your shoulder will turn a little: do not panic! This turn is vital, since it is your shoulders that will determine the direction and timing – and therefore the power – of the shot.
- Remember that the essence of the drive is a swing, not a punch.
- On impact, your hands must be over the ball, arms straight and wrists slightly cocked to keep the bat straight.
- Hit through the line of the ball. Now relive the sweet sound of willow cracking into leather, and enjoy the applause.

COMING DOWN THE WICKET

Changing the bowler's length is one of your most valuable weapons, in all forms of the game; and coming down the pitch is one of the best ways of doing this. The chassis, the shimmy, the glide, the two-step, going on the charge, hopping out, running down the wicket: call it what you will, but coming down the wicket has proved its worth over and over again, whether against Test match spinners or medium-pacers in a one-day match.

They say you might as well be stumped by 5 yards as by 5 inches, and there is some wisdom in this: if you are going to come down the pitch, do so boldly, and remember that you are doing it not to escape from a bowler, but to intimidate him. You are the hunter, not the prey. Five yards down the track, you are sending out a very aggressive signal, and you will definitely force the bowler to change his length and rethink his approach.

Playing the shot

When you come down the wicket, do so at the ball: begin your movement the instant the ball leaves the bowler's hand. Come down slowly to begin with and be prepared to defend if you have to, without forgetting that your intent is aggressive. If (and only if!) the ball is in the correct place, can you then hit it safely over the top or along the ground. Above all, keep your head still and watch the ball throughout: it's easy for beginners to let their heads roll back as they 'tee off', usually resulting in a mis-hit or a complete miss.

There are a number of methods of coming down the wicket, ranging from the chassis and the glide to a slow walk down the pitch with the bat in the ready position. Some players simply run down. However, the sequence illustrated here represents a more conventional approach.

Your first movement is important: the first stride with your front foot will determine how far you go. Don't be timid in this respect: make sure you come a long way down the wicket, pointing your shoulder towards where you expect the ball to pitch (1). Obviously your height will determine how far your front foot can move: tall batsmen will need to measure or restrict their stride, while shorter players can stretch out. Experiment and find the best method for you.

Frame 2 shows the 'slide', the feet coming close together. This is easier than picking up the feet, but it has two major drawbacks: firstly, your head will come over its original height, which will distort your view of the ball and interfere with your judgement of its flight; and secondly, the shuffle limits the distance you can advance down the pitch.

Here the batsman has crossed his back foot behind his front foot, a movement called the 'chassis' (3). This means that when he reaches out with his front foot to the pitch of the ball, he'll have an extra six inches at his disposal. This method also helps to keep the eyes and head level, which preserves the batsman's set-up and helps him play correctly, both then attacking and defending.

One of the disadvantages of using this 'cross-over' method is that it can take you to the leg side of the ball and away from the line; and if the bowler sees you coming, he might be able to adjust and bowl the ball just wide of your reach, exposing you to a stumping.

Frames 4 and 5 show the completion of the shot, as the weight is once again transferred forward, in this case into an attacking stroke. Notice how far the front foot has come from its starting point in the first frame: by staying nimble, the batter has advanced a good three feet up the track, radically disrupting the bowler's length.

Common problems with coming down the wicket

- **It's going straight up in the air:** players who have had success in the past with coming down the wicket suddenly find that when they go for the big shot they end up skying the ball and being caught. This is purely a problem of timing and co-ordination: the batsman is getting under the ball rather than hitting it. Remember, as you get into the shot, you must rotate the front shoulder so that your hands can swing through the ball. If you don't rotate your shoulder, you will find that the bottom hand will come through the shot far too quickly, and the ball will go straight up in the air. As mentioned many times already, the bottom hand is key to hitting the ball a long way: anyone who's hit high catches at fielding practices will know this. So whether you are hitting over the top or trying to clear the field, it is important that the bottom hand is working properly to provide power and timing in the shot.

- **I'm not getting to the ball:** footwork is the most important aspect of coming down the pitch – more specifically, the distance between your front foot and your back foot. If you make small, hesitant movements, you aren't going to get to the correct hitting area. If the ball is turning, swinging or seaming, and you're stranded short of where you need to be, you're going to be in trouble. If this happens, quickly try to find a way to bale out of the situation: sometimes the only solution is to try to stop the ball, and hasten back to your crease.

THROWING THE KITCHEN SINK AT IT

It's worth remembering that just because you are coming down the pitch, it doesn't mean you have to hit the ball out of the ground. If the bowler sees you advancing and changes his length, you are perfectly entitled – and in fact required – to play defensively if the ball is not there to hit. This is why it is important that you do not give any visual clues as to when you might be leaving the crease, but rather advance after the ball has been released.

Indeed, dummying and coming down the pitch are all part of the game when trying to upset a spinner's length; but many batsmen don't practise this skill, and are therefore uncomfortable doing it in match conditions. Just like any skill, it is vital that you practise and gain confidence.

If the ball is a half-volley, then go ahead and hit it: your momentum will carry it a long way. If you want to hit it for six, lean back slightly, get the hands underneath the ball, and carry them right the way through. Here it's forgivable if the bottom hand overtakes the top hand, since you're trying to gain upward momentum. In fact, when you decide to unleash the bottom hand, give it the 'kitchen sink' treatment – don't choke or give up on the shot before it's gone all the way through.

Be careful, though, of trying to hit it too hard: you can get too far underneath the ball.

4. FRONT-FOOT GLANCE

The leg glance off the front foot, while not glamorous, is a useful one to have in your repertoire of strokes. The Nawab of Pataudi and the great Ranjitsinjhi were famous for using variations of this shot, and it stood them in good stead: the wristy glance is an effective way of harvesting steady runs by working the ball around, and more specifically, working it backward of square on the leg side.

When to play the shot

The front-foot glance is best employed when you are receiving deliveries of a fairly full length on your pads, or fractionally outside of them on the leg side. Anything along this line is essentially a risk-free single begging to be taken. Alternatively, it can be a manufactured stroke in the context of a one-day game, working a straighter delivery fine on the leg side to take advantage of fine leg being up in the circle. In general, it is a safe stroke to any delivery that comes in to you, whether an inswinger or an off-spinner bowling to a right-handed batsman.

Playing the shot

Go forward as you would for a forward defensive stroke: your head should be right over your front foot, with your weight going forward (1). As the ball swings in, bring the bat down in front of the pad, and rotate the wrists towards the leg side and slightly downwards (in order to angle the ball onto the ground) (2). Control the bat with your top hand, and allow your bottom hand to take the soft route, with only two fingers on the handle so that the bat can be turned without obstruction, glancing the ball off the face and away for a handy single (3, 4 and 5).

Be aware of your balance when playing this stroke: less experienced batsmen often topple forward if they miss the ball, which can be a gift to the alert wicket-keeper, lurking in the hope of a stumping down the leg side. Remember to keep the bat upright and in line: if you play across the ball, you risk getting a leading edge (which will carry to the bowler, especially if you've twisted the bat hard in your hands) or being given out LBW.

5. THE PICK-UP

The pick-up is the glamorous cousin of the leg glance. If the traditional front-foot glance is all about wrists, timing and balance, then the pick-up is all about brute strength and an overpowering bottom hand.

Playing the shot

The easiest way to explain the wrist action of this shot is to point to a tennis forehand loaded with top-spin. Bring your feet together, wait for the ball to arrive under your eyes on or outside leg stump, and then launch it behind square with a strong flick of your wrists, almost as if you were trying to impart top-spin on the ball. Gary Kirsten used the shot to great effect in the 1996 World Cup in Asia: on slow pitches, against spinners and medium-pacers (most memorably the part-timers of the United Arab Emirates), Kirsten peppered the mid-wicket and deep-backward-square boundaries by picking up anything bowled at a suitable length, including balls on or outside his off stump.

6. THE BACK-FOOT DRIVE

It may seem incongruous to group this stroke here, along with front-foot drives and pick-ups, but the back-foot drive is something of an anomaly among cricketing shots. It is the only attacking stroke played off the back foot with a straight bat, and it therefore bridges the divide between the attacking front-foot shots played with straight bats, and the attacking back-foot shots played with horizontal bats.

The back-foot drive played well is almost always a sign of a very good (or even great) batsman. Bowlers in the top echelons of the game are getting stronger, fitter and faster all the time, and to score off them, given the miserly lengths they bowl, takes some doing. The back-foot drive, or 'back drive' as it is also known, allows those few batsmen who have mastered it to help themselves to more runs than the fast bowlers of the world would like. But it takes superb judgement of length and excellent control of both hands to pilfer short and nasty stuff for runs while forcing off the back foot.

When to play the shot

The back drive is played to a ball that pitches short of a good length, but relatively close to the body, giving no room to cut. Be certain that you are mentally and physically prepared before you start trying to play it: first get your eye in and get accustomed to the pace and bounce of the pitch – otherwise any extra bounce could take the outside edge.

Playing the shot

1. Start to turn your front shoulder towards the ball as it comes at you. 2. Turn your shoulders fully round with your backswing, and be ready to hit the ball hard once you've identified whether or not the back drive is a viable shot for the delivery. Move your back foot back and across in line with middle- and off stump, with the toes pointing to backward point. 3. Bring your bat down to intersect with the line of the delivery. Keep your front elbow high, the bat remaining close to your body, and let your front arm lead the shot. Stay balanced, with a still head and eyes fixed firmly on the ball. 4. Hit the ball under your eyes. The elbows of both arms should make a cradling movement, as if you are rocking a baby vertically. 5. Follow through with a controlled punch, like the check drive on the front foot. Keep the bat on the line of the ball, and go up on the toes of the back foot to give more emphasis to the shot.

Practising the shot

As with the front-foot drives, progressive training can build the shot into your armoury until it becomes second nature. Use a stationary ball at stump height, first to learn the basic principles of the shoulder, arm and hand movements. Then add in foot movements, and then enlist a partner to throw a ball underarm from the usual length – which in the case of the back drive is about six to eight metres from the bat. This is the ideal way to practise, as most pitches (apart from concrete) have varying bounce, and without consistent bounce while practising this shot, you can become extremely frustrated.

Common problems with the back drive

- The most common fault associated with the back drive is the inability of some batsmen to play the stroke with bent arms in the 'cradle' formation (left) because of the height of the ball. In these cases the body opens up and becomes too square on, which in turn prevents the bat from following the correct line.
- Secondly, some batsmen assume that because the ball generally goes quite square off a back drive, they need to play it square. This is not the case: the natural angle of the stroke – even one aimed at mid-off – will take the ball square; and trying to help it can only make you vulnerable to getting an edge and being caught behind.
- Most successful back-foot drivers have powerful arms and upper bodies: judicious weight training can help to make you a better driver off the back foot.

The 'cradle' formation: imagine rocking a baby in your arms, but now turn the baby so that it stands upright.

CROSS-BAT SHOTS

THE CUTS

'Sunshine, thou should not cut until July!'

So said the legendary Yorkshireman Wilfred Rhodes, giving (presumably unsolicited) advice to a young player who played a cut too early in the season. What Rhodes meant was that playing cut shots was a dangerous business until pitches dried out and became firm in the summer sun, and the ball started coming onto the bat. Today it remains a dangerous shot if not played correctly, but one that is highly productive if practised.

It is a shot that has spawned numerous variations: cuts off the back and front foot, the late cut (favoured by so many in the early 1900s), and more recently the upper cut, slicing fast bowling over the slips and away towards third man. This shot in particular was born of desperate times, as Tony Greig and Alan Knott tried to find ways of scoring off Lillee and Thomson on the ferocious pitches of Australia that didn't involve hooking, pulling, or getting in line more than was absolutely necessary!

Even the apparently formal, traditional variations of the shot have been adapted and experimented with over the years: the late great Denis Compton used to give himself room by moving his back foot outside leg stump to a straightish delivery, and cutting on length rather than line.

But if there is one general piece of advice that holds true for most types of cut, it is that offered by the stalwart South African batsman, Peter Kirsten, when Bob Woolmer asked him what made him such a good cutter. 'If you're going to cut, cut hard,' was his reply.

This advice is worth following: if the ball is rising, follow the rise and cut up. If the ball is levelling off or dropping, cut accordingly.

1. SQUARE CUT OFF THE BACK FOOT

This is a great run-scoring shot, both fun and tricky to play, but it is also a dangerous stroke that induces a large number of dismissals, with the batsman often out caught in the gully or the slips. So play it sparingly, and only to deliveries that are conducive to the cut shot. As with all cross-batted shots, be wary of attempting it on pitches of uneven bounce. Remember to keep the bat parallel to the ground: if you don't, the shot becomes even more risky than it is already.

When to play the shot

The cut is played to a short ball that is at least an arm's length outside off stump when it reaches the crease. If it's a delivery from a pace bowler, you need to craft the shot entirely from gentle timing. If you're facing a slow bowler, hit it as hard as you can. But in both cases, make sure that you've chosen a short ball that gives you enough time to get into the correct position: arms fully extended, a yard away from you.

Playing the square cut off the back foot

1. As you recognize the ball to cut, you should start turning your front shoulder towards it, which initiates the back foot's movement. 2. Your back foot should move across the pitch and ideally your toes should point down towards third man. This allows you to hold the correct shape, and to get the right hip out of the way. At the same time, your hands should be in position above shoulder-height, which will allow the correct bat path during the shot. 3. Make contact with the ball at arm's length for maximum effect and power. Your weight must transfer from the front foot onto the back foot, and the back knee needs to bend slightly for control. This is the toughest part of the shot to master (and to coach), as the final part of the shot relies on a quick wristy rotation of the hands commonly referred to as 'rolling the wrists'. 4 and 5. The start and end of the shot are similar in that the arms are bent on impact, straightened to guide the ball, and then bent again. As the shot finishes, focus on keeping your shoulders square to the ball as your hands and arms do the work.

2. SQUARE CUT OFF THE FRONT FOOT

As with the square cut off the back foot, this shot is played to a wide, short ball outside the off stump, normally on good wickets when the batsman is set and ready.

Playing the square cut off the front foot

This variation of the cut uses very similar arm and wrist movements to the cut off the back foot. Move your front foot across the stumps so that it points to cover: this will ensure that the front shoulder has turned in order to allow your arms to swing.

Keep the bottom hand above the top hand as the bat moves into position to strike the ball: this will keep the bat parallel to the ground. At the point of contact, keep your arms straight and your weight over your front leg. Immediately after contact, roll your wrists.

The full follow-through ensures that there is no body turn. If you have completed the shot correctly, the bat handle will be pointing in the direction of the ball.

3. THE LATE CUT

The late cut is one of the more delicate shots, and although it is no longer as popular as it once was, it remains a thing of beauty whenever it is played. In tactical terms, the late cut is almost identical to the reverse dab (a delicate reverse sweep).

When to play the shot

The late cut is played to deliveries just wide of off stump that are too full to play at with any of the more conventional cut shots. The batsman also needs some pace on the ball: the spinners' arm-ball is often the ideal delivery at which to play the late cut. It is often the safest and most rewarding shot to play to a spinner or medium-pacer when there are no slips in place and the keeper is standing up: guiding the ball almost out of his gloves past off stump and down to third man for a single is delightfully cheeky, as demonstrated often by Pakistan's Javed Miandad.

Some coaches warn against late-cutting off-spinners, instead recommending that the shot be reserved for balls that are short of a length and headed towards third man. On tracks that offer the off-spinner plenty of turn they might have a point, but on a flat track with little turn, it can be extremely lucrative to late-cut the off-spinner.

Playing the late cut

1 and 2. The back foot goes back and inside the line of the ball. 3–5. Lower your body by bending your knees, as the further the ball is pitched up, the lower it will stay. Keep your eyes locked on the ball, as this is a shot based entirely on timing – try to play the ball as late as possible, so you're almost dabbing it out of the wicket-keeper's hands. The actual strike should resemble a tapping motion, as though knocking a stump into the ground with the face of the bat. Wait and let the ball go past your body: you'll be amazed at how much time you have. Once you've spotted the gap between backward point and the keeper, use the pace of the ball to run it down to third man with soft hands. When the ball bounces lower (or higher) than the knees, bend to adjust to that height. The secret is to keep your hands above the ball.

PRACTISING THE SHOT

The late cut is not easy to practise unless you have a true surface like concrete or carpet. However, with the help of two friends, you can get the feel of the shot well enough: ask one to throw to you on a good length a foot outside your off stump, and get the other to play wicket-keeper. Without alarming the volunteer behind the stumps too much, work on trying to tap the ball down gently just before it reaches his hands, with your back foot pointing at him.

Common problems with cutting

- **Uneven bounce:** poor or uneven pitches make cutting dangerous, as the slightest variation in bounce can cause you to top-edge a cut behind the wicket, or bottom-edge the ball into your stumps.
- **Poor body position and poor use of the arms:** the mechanics of the cut shot are very specific, and many players see the stroke merely as an opportunity to lash out square on the off side, without paying due care to the role of their bottom hand, the rotation of their shoulders, and the position of their feet. Study the two sequences below.

Notice how in the first, poor foot and shoulder positions cause the batter to hit over the ball by many inches. In the second, the back foot goes further to the off side, while the toes point at gully, rather than backward point. This helps the hips rotate further, which in turn helps the shoulders to rotate better. The result: a crisp, cracking cut.

- **Wrists don't rotate:** the power, timing and placement of the cut shot comes from the rapid rotation of the wrists at the point of impact, not from the swing of the arms. In fact, there should be negligible arm movement in the stroke, and the wrists should be allowed to whip through, rather like cracking a whip.

If the second and third problems continue to dog you, and you continue to be dismissed when you play cuts, perhaps eliminate the shot from your repertoire until you have spent more time practising it.

THE HOOK AND THE PULL

There still seems to be some confusion in the minds of many players and junior coaches as to the difference between the hook and the pull, and a brief distinction should be drawn here.

The hook is played to a bouncer or a ball aimed above chest height. Hooking usually sends the ball behind square, but this will also depend on the line of the ball as it is delivered: the straighter and faster the delivery, the finer you will have to hook it. Likewise, if is outside off stump, it is possible to hook it in front of square.

The pull, on the other hand, is played to a ball that is shorter and usually slower, and as such, the foot movements required of the pull are easier to manage. For example, the pull is often used against spinners or medium-pacers who have dropped one short.

Both shots, however, are played with straight, fairly rigid arms, which provide the power and the control.

1. THE HOOK

The hook shot can be played to a bouncer or short-pitched delivery aimed at your head. It is an extremely risky shot, and you must be confident that you can cope before you attempt it; once you play this shot to a fast bowler, you have thrown down the gauntlet and you can expect him to bowl you a few more bouncers – or alternatively, change his length and pitch the ball up more.

The success of the hook shot is often dictated by the height of the ball. The higher the ball when it reaches you, the more likely it is to rocket up off the face or back of the bat, providing a catch for the wicket-keeper, or – as bats gets heavier and meatier – a high catch for fine leg or third man.

Playing the shot

Hooking requires perfect concentration. Watch the ball as it comes to you. Keep your head and eyes very still. Do not blink, flinch or look away! The moment you take your eyes off the ball, you are effectively blind and a sitting duck, liable to be hit on the helmet or the back of the neck.

1–3. The first movement for the hook shot sees the back foot going back and just outside the line of the ball. The front foot then joins the back foot, but has no weight on it and can lift off the ground easily and move in conjunction with the swing of the bat. Keep your balance slightly forwards of the centre of your body, and try to position the shoulder inside the line of delivery, with your hands as high as possible in the backswing. As you move backwards, extend your lower arm as far in front of you as possible, and retract the top hand by flexing the elbow of the upper arm. 4. Make contact in front of your eyes with arms held out straight, while your whole chest pivots around, followed by your legs and feet. If possible, try to hit the ball just inside the line of your head, to avoid injury should you miss or deflect the delivery back towards you. 5. Follow through by spinning like a ballerina in Swan Lake! And to make sure you don't end up a dead duck, try to hit down on the ball as you swivel. Sometimes if the ball grows too 'big' on you, this will be impossible, but most balls of chest-height can be controlled in this way.

Practising the shot

Start with tennis balls, and have your coach or a friend throw them accurately at your head from about 10 metres away. Gradually increase the pace and then move on to the hard ball. Add a helmet for protection when doing this, and be prepared for the odd knock. Move onto overarm throwing, and then finally to a bowling machine. Increase the pace and make sure that you watch the ball all the way.

Common problems with hooking

- **Hitting the ball too hard:** if the hands move too quickly through the line of the ball (which can happen when you're pumped up and playing for your life against a pumped-up paceman), you can end up mistiming or splicing the ball to a nearby fielder. Or, in the worst-case scenario, you can be through the shot too soon, and take a painful blow to the body.

  You can combat this by being in control of the shot from start to finish. Rather than hitting the ball, concentrate on helping it round, using the pace of the ball rather than your own speed and strength. This is another distinction between hooking and pulling: when you pull, you hit the ball; but when you hook, you simply help it on its way.

- **Playing at balls bouncing too high:** some batsmen have a reputation for being 'happy hookers', players who compulsively chase short balls around their shoulders and faces. Bowlers mark them down for special treatment, and, if the umpire isn't being particularly strict, the bouncers start flying.

  If you find yourself halfway into a hook shot to a ball that has suddenly got too big on you, the most important thing to do is to get the bat out of the path of the ball: either raise or lower your arms, just as long as your bat isn't near the ball. Alternatively, bale out of the shot by bowing your head and simultaneously swinging your hands down very quickly as you turn, allowing the ball to go over your head. If neither of these options is available, get your bat out of the way, close your eyes and think of Brian Close, and take it on the body for the good of your team!

- **Old-fashioned stomach-churning fear:** nobody wants to get hit, especially not in the face or on the head, and sometimes batsmen flinch or look down as they play this stroke, usually with exactly the results they feared! Remember, if you are wearing a helmet, playing a hook shot is not likely to be lethal. Always wear your helmet when practising this shot as well as playing.

  If you intend continuing to play the hook shot, try to learn the signs that bowlers give off when they are about to bowl a bouncer: some have a faster run-up, others call codes to their captain, others just look very keyed-up and seem to be exuding fire and brimstone! And there's always the telltale sign of two fielders posted out for the hook behind the wicket.

TO HOOK OR NOT TO HOOK?

Steve Waugh decided to stop hooking altogether, as did his brother Mark. Bob Simpson, one of Australia's best batsmen, once gave Steve Waugh some interesting advice: 'You do not necessarily have to look good against fast bowling – the secret is to survive it!'

Viv Richards used to go for the hook straight away to unsettle the bowler and show his mental strength. During World Series cricket in 1978, Australian speedster Len Pascoe bounced Richards at the beginning of the innings – in his own words, 'to attempt to unsettle him'. Viv took him on and smacked ball after ball to the leg boundary. Ian Chappell pointed out to the bowler that Viv was enjoying this passage of play and suggested that Pascoe pitch it up to him instead. The bowler did so, and Viv calmly smacked him back over his head for four more – a classic duel of tactics and dominance.

The real trick is to pick the right kind of surfaces (even and true bounce) and the right pace of those bowlers who are 'hookable'. Avoid hooking really fast bowlers – but if you decide you want to take them on with this shot, wait until they are tired.

2. THE PULL

Playing the pull shot well from an early age will give the young batter a big advantage. Most young bowlers tend to drift down the leg side and bowl short, inviting the pull shot. At higher levels of the game, playing the pull shot is more often than not dictated by a field setting that favours the off side. The batsman then looks at ways of manipulating the ball into areas where runs are more freely available.

Playing the pull is probably the most natural shot in the game. You swing as though chopping down a tree, smacking a blanket or a rug hanging on a washing line. In fact many coaches, when teaching a youngster to play for the first time, start by teaching the pull, which always stimulates young batsmen. It's fun to hit the ball hard!

When to play the shot

This shot is played to a short ball (commonly called a 'long-hop') delivered by a medium-pace or slow bowler, going down the leg side at waist height.

The shot may also be played to a slow short ball pitching outside the off stump. This is a bad delivery and the batsman should take full advantage by putting it away to the boundary.

Playing the shot

Remember the fourth principle of batting: 'Move your feet into the correct position.' In order to play the pull shot both well and successfully, the feet need to move into position quickly, establishing a firm base.

1. The first movement takes the back foot back and towards the middle or leg stump, making sure that you go back onto the toe of that foot (which should be pointing up the pitch or towards mid-off). This enables you to pivot, allowing the front foot to move out towards the square leg umpire. 2. To make sure the ball is hit hard, the backswing has to be high and full. Contact has to be made in front of the eyes, so the head must move into line. Foot movements enable this; the wider the ball, the wider the front foot movement. The toes of the front and back feet should end up parallel to the return crease. This will ensure that the ball can be hit in front of the wicket (square leg). 3 and 4. The bat should make contact with the ball in front of the eyes: on contact, the arms should be straight for maximum power. Immediately after contact, roll the wrists to keep the ball on the ground. 5. The final part of the shot is the follow-through. Weight should transfer from the back to the front foot to keep the ball down and to ensure maximum power.

Practising the shot

Once again, progression training is key. In this case, try using a ball on a stump, as illustrated below: get the position right, then the feet, then the whole movement, and then graduate to tennis- and cricket balls.

Common problems with pulling

The most common error that creeps into the pull shot is that foot movements are too slow, and therefore do not get the head in line with the ball. Making contact with bent arms and the weight remaining on the back foot also reduces power, with the ball being mis-hit up in the air.

An important element of the pull shot is to make sure that the bat is parallel to the ground, not at an angle. It's a common mistake to have the bat at a 45° angle, which increases the risk of top-edging the ball into your face. As in any run-scoring shot, if you do not feel right at the last moment, bail out of the shot and aim to survive.

Generally, however, the pull is one of the easier cricket shots to play. For this reason, it is a handy basic shot to teach at junior level, as it will enable younger players to score runs.

THE SWEEP SHOTS

If you want to force the spinner to change his length, but you don't want to advance down the wicket and risk a stumping, sweeping can be the way to go.

Jonty Rhodes

Rhodes's point here is something all batters must bear in mind, rather than taking unnecessary risks: the sweep's primary objective is to change the bowler's length.

Despite what a dwindling pool of die-hard sceptics might say, the sweep is a genuine cricket shot. It has a proud and growing pedigree, as more and more batsmen both great and ordinary hone and practise it. By now, it has been used on dozens of occasions to destroy bowling attacks, specifically those based on spin.

Mike Gatting's ill-fated reverse sweep in the 1987 World Cup final against Australia is still held up by critics of both the reverse sweep and its slightly more respectable sibling, the standard sweep, as an example of why it is dangerous. What is seldom mentioned, however, is that Gatting tried the shot on the very first ball he faced from new bowler Allan Border. Was the demise of Gatting – and eventually England – the result of the sweep, or of a batsman not taking time to get used to a new bowler? Likewise, nobody mentions Graham Gooch sweeping his way to 80 in a World Cup semi-final against Pakistan, or Gordon Greenidge using the shot to win a Test against England with an over to spare, after David Gower had been criticized for declaring too late.

However, despite these successes, it is hard to deny that the sweep is a higher-risk shot than most: first, because you're always taking a chance playing across the line;

and second, because certain umpires have decided that it's an inherently risky and unwise stroke, and are more inclined to listen to the appeals of bowlers when you're sweeping than to judge their appeals on merit.

But ask any spin bowler what he thinks of the sweep, and he will tell you that it does have the effect of messing up his length, and if played well, it can make it very difficult for him to contain the batsman. Because the sweep is played to a good length ball, it reduces the bowler's options, forcing him to bowl more quickly or slowly, which in turn forces him to change his length. Remember, you're sweeping to force him to change his length: it's no use sweeping once an over and leaving him settled for five balls out of six.

Heave-ho!

Any cross-batted shot into the leg side has the potential to reach or clear the ropes for a four or six, and to many young batsmen, the sweep seems an invitation to try for a boundary. Bob Woolmer encouraged batsmen who played sweep shots to hit down: the object is to change the bowler's length, and scoring a boundary keeps you on a strike and gives the bowler a chance to settle.

However, you can sweep the ball to the boundary, whether with a violently hit conventional sweep or the more glamorous slog sweep. Australia's Matthew Hayden is a prime example of someone who has perfected what can be called the 'bludgeon

WITH OR AGAINST SPIN?

The principle behind lifting the ball into the stands is the subject of ongoing debate: namely, do you hit with the spin, or against it?

All the good sweepers will tell you that it's safer to hit against the spin. Their reasoning? You are hitting into the 'final' line of the ball, in other words, the line the ball is going to take until it hits your bat, as opposed to a line going (infinitely far) away from your bat as the ball spins away.

The mechanics of this were touched on earlier, when discussing how best to alter your stance when facing a leg-spinner pitching it out of the rough, but it bears repeating. When you sweep, there is a natural tendency to rush your wrists through the shot as you see the ball turning. The result is that the bat overtakes the ball, and you can end up top-edging as you rush under the delivery, bottom-edging as you skim the top of it, or even lobbing the most embarrassing of catches up off the back of the bat.

In short, if you sweep with the spin, make sure that you smother the spin by hitting down on top of it.

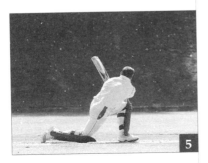

sweep': a conventional, technically correct sweep, hit extremely hard. Throwing the kitchen sink into the shot has two advantages: firstly, and obviously, it has the power behind it to take it to the boundary and beat any outfielders who might run down a ball rolling more slowly; and secondly, it almost automatically removes short leg from the equation. Most short legs are simply not fast (or brave!) enough to get down to a ball hit that hard, which usually leads to the man being removed, and the pressure on the batsman being lifted.

In order to sweep the ball for six, you need to get into a position that allows you to hit the ball into the air. This technique – the above-mentioned slog sweep – is discussed on pp. 81–2.

Malice aforethought

Many coaches and critics criticize the sweep for being a premeditated shot. But it has to be: it is an attack on the bowler, rather than a response to a specific delivery.

Of course, it is dangerous to play it too early, since the bowler will be able to adjust, whether by bowling more quickly (the arm ball) or more slowly (to create more bounce), both of which will make the sweep shot much more difficult. In these cases it's important that you have a form of counter-attack, such as the defensive sweep, described on p. 80.

However, an early movement into the shot, with the back knee already on the ground as the ball leaves the bowler's hand, will allow you to move the front foot around according to whichever sweep you need to play. For example, if you place the front foot inside the line (i.e., the off side) of the line of the ball, you will be able to guide the ball fine. If you stay on the leg side of the ball, you will be able to hit the ball squarer, and so on.

1. ORTHODOX SWEEP

When to play the orthodox sweep

Former England captain Mike Brearley summed it up nicely: 'On an excellent pitch, it's folly to play the sweep when runs can freely be had by driving; but on a "turner" or a pitch where the ball does not come on for the drive, the sweep may be the most effective, even the safest shot.'

It is important when learning to play the sweep that you identify the length you should play the full sweep to. If you reach out in front of you with both hands on the bat and touch the ground, you will see the best position for the ball to pitch. Play to the length of the ball – in other words, the length you'd also normally consider a forward defence.

Playing the orthodox sweep

Study the sequence on the opposite page together with this front-on sequence for a clearer picture of the correct technique for the sweep shot. **1.** Make sure that the position you get into is comfortable and has a solid base, so that when you swing the bat, the shot will be balanced and controlled. The height of the bat swing depends on how hard you want to hit the ball. Here the batsman is looking for the full sweep. **2.** Note the position of the back knee and the front foot: the knee is just inside the line of the front foot to create balance. The front leg is almost vertical, and the head is over the top of the front knee. **3.** Swing the bat parallel to the ground, keeping the head forward. **4.** Make contact with the ball with your bat parallel to the ground, and your arms as near to parallel as you can manage without losing control or power. Your arms should also be at full strength now for maximum power in the shot. Also notice that the head has now moved slightly forward over the knee. At the point of impact, the bottom hand's wrist rolls over the top hand, and the arms will begin to bend and swing over the front shoulder. If you have swung the bat correctly from the very first position of the swing (1), your follow-through should look like that in 5 in the side-on sequence.

Common problems with sweeping

When troubleshooting the sweep shot, two problems keep cropping up.

- **The head stays behind the knee.** Instead of pushing their weight forward and reaching a balanced position on their back knee, batters tend to hang back, going down onto their pad with the head still in the position shown in 1.
- **The bat is held at too great an angle to the ground.** The ideal sweep shot has the bat sweeping past across the line of the delivery almost exactly parallel to the ground. However, many batters bring the bat through at 30 or 45 degrees to the ground, which means they have no control over the shot, and greatly increase the risk of a top edge popping up, either to the wicket-keeper or close fielder, or into their own faces.

2. DEFENSIVE SWEEP

There are many varieties of sweep, and a particularly useful variation of the orthodox sweep is the defensive sweep, sometimes referred to as a paddle. The shot was christened the 'defensive sweep' by Alan Knott, who became a fine exponent of it. He used it simply as an option for picking up singles very fine down the leg side, but it can be used to good effect in the one-day game: with fine leg up, it can run away for four.

When to play the defensive sweep

Good spin bowlers will work as hard at undoing you as you are working at undoing them. Sometimes – especially if you've premeditated the sweep and have made a miscalculation – you can find yourself beaten by flight or spin, thoroughly committed to the orthodox sweep, and more or less stranded unless you take sudden action. That action is the defensive sweep.

A good example of this is when you've gone down to sweep, and the bowler has slipped in a fuller, quicker arm-ball, and you're staring down the barrel of a potential LBW appeal.

Playing the defensive sweep

The set-up position and early execution are identical to those of the orthodox sweep as outlined above (1 and 2); but instead of hitting out at the ball, pull your hands back, as close to your front foot as possible. Lay the back of the bat on the ground, and angle the face to where you want the ball to go (3, 4 and 5).

The ball will then slide off the face down to short leg, the pace of delivery – rather than your arms – providing the momentum.

The defensive sweep is very much a get-out-of-jail shot, but it can be used intelligently – and cheekily – to score runs where there are not usually any fielders.

The reverse defensive sweep (see sequence below) gives you the option to score on the off side in similar situations: simply change the angle of the bat.

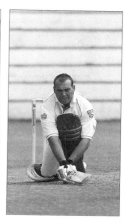

3. SLOG SWEEP

Hitting a sweep shot for six requires a different body position, since you need to create more room for your hands and arms. Don't forget that every time you lift the ball into the air, you're at risk.

When to play the slog sweep

This shot is played when you want to hit the ball over the infield with the intention of sending it for six. Sometimes, it is played to score much-needed runs as fast as possible during a hectic run chase; at other times, it is used to gain a psychological edge over a bowler, or to remove him from the attack entirely. Hansie Cronje was one of the first international batsmen to perfect the shot, and when he used it against the much feared Shane Warne in 1993, the runs he scored were far outweighed by the sense that South Africa wasn't entirely in awe of the Australian.

Likewise, in 1998, Cronje went after Muttiah Muralitharan, probably the best off-spinner the world has ever seen, slog-sweeping him to all corners of Centurion Park. Muralitharan was taken to the cleaners, and Cronje went to what was the fastest 50 in Test history at that time. His runs greatly helped South Africa's cause, but the dominance he asserted over the Sri Lankan strike bowler was much more important.

Playing the slog sweep

The slog sweep is an extension of the sweep played to a ball wider of the leg stump. In other words, you're always hitting against the spin, either to a leg-spinner or an orthodox left-arm spinner. Left-handers slog-sweep off-spinners.

Splay your front leg out towards the leg side (1). This allows room for the arms and hands to get under the ball. Keep your arms straight, in order to maximize power in the shot (2 and 3). Then follow through expansively: don't check the shot or stop the bat in line with your front knee (4 and 5). If struck correctly, they'll be looking for the ball twelve rows back.

4. REVERSE SWEEP

It's worth pausing for a moment to discuss why this shot crawled out of the woodwork, why it causes so much consternation, and how it came to be accepted (more or less) as part of the game.

The first myth that needs debunking is that the reverse sweep is a very recent innovation. This is simply not true: it has been used since the early 1970s, and perhaps even earlier. Mushtaq Mohammed played it against Bob Woolmer's swing bowling, and Gordon Greenidge used it to great effect in the 1976 Jubilee Test, playing for the Rest of the World.

It was Dermott Reeve, however, who made it famous (or infamous), when he used it as a tactical weapon to break the fielding regulations that were stifling English one-day cricket in the early 1990s.

At that time, one-day international cricket regulations had recognized the need for a free flow of runs, and had restricted the number of men permitted on the leg side to just five. However, English one-day cricket had not yet adopted this rule, and an off-spinner could bowl at leg stump with as many as seven men on the leg side.

Not surprisingly, it was extremely difficult to score against this kind of tactic. Reeve simply exploited this convention by playing the reverse sweep, forcing the field to change accordingly. Little did he know how well his unorthodox shot would work, or what the ramifications would be.

Bob Woolmer (then the Warwickshire coach) and Reeve decided to let the entire team practise the shot, and Reeve endorsed the tactic in a team meeting. Woolmer was in complete agreement, and set about working out how best to teach the shot.

Unfortunately this decision didn't reach Warwickshire's second eleven coach Neal Abberley: Bob Woolmer remembered wandering over to the nets one day to see a tearful Roger Twose stomping away across the tarmac. Woolmer asked what the problem was, and was told that Abberley had expelled him from the net for practising the reverse sweep!

Woolmer apologized to Abberley for the breakdown in communication, but he recalled that although his colleague accepted his apology, he couldn't help feeling that Abberley was initially dead set against the shot.

Woolmer himself had doubts, but Reeve was a good salesman. When the time came to put the plan into action, it had an immediate impact: the opposition's disdain for the shot saw Warwickshire exploit it to the maximum for two years. During this time visiting sides came and went with the attitude that Reeve's team were lucky, insane, stupid, crazy – Woolmer heard it all.

The result for Warwickshire was a Nat-West trophy at Lords in 1993, two out of three one-day trophies in 1993, and the championship and two more trophies in 1995, the year after Woolmer left the county to coach South Africa.

The statistics speak for themselves. During those years, Warwickshire managed on many occasions to score at over six runs an over against spin – three runs an over more than their opposition. If ten overs were bowled by spinners, that translated into a 30-run advantage.

Woolmer's departure, and Reeve's retirement, saw Warwickshire gradually stop using the sweep, and the lessons learnt were either forgotten or abandoned. When Woolmer returned in 2000, he found reverse-sweeping dead and buried as a tactic, and sweeping in general so discouraged that the level of one-day cricket played had regressed.

However, when English teams did finally accept one-day international rules, the shot – and the sweep in general – did become less effective, partly because it was now an option open to all. It remains a very useful means of disrupting bowlers and upsetting teams.

When to play the reverse sweep

The shot is best employed against a good-length ball, usually (but not necessarily) outside the off stump, against a bowler defending the leg side.

Ideally, there should be a gap behind square on the off side, around backward point. With the reverse sweep, you're looking to sweep the ball through that gap.

Playing the reverse sweep

The early movements in the shot are basically those of the orthodox sweep (1). However, these are followed by a turnover: the bottom hand comes directly over the top hand (2), and the face of the bat turns towards the off side.

The grip dictates that the shot starts from the leg side, with the bat following through to the off side (3, 4 and 5). This sequence ends before the follow-through, but the reverse-sweep follow-through can be just as expansive as that of the conventional sweep.

Variations

The front leg can get in the way of the hands, as can be seen above, so you might want to experiment with some other variations.

1. **Start with both feet in the crease and open up the stance.** Place the back foot down the pitch, as if you're about to hit a two-handed backhand in tennis or squash (make sure that the front foot stays behind the batting crease to prevent the stumping). Now hit across the line, bat parallel to the ground. This is the method originally used by Dermott Reeve and Jonty Rhodes.

2. **Rhodes gradually altered how he played the shot, and ended up reverse-sweeping as follows.** He jumped into the backhand squash position – effectively taking up

the stance of a left-hander – making sure both feet were inside the crease. Now he could either play the reverse sweep, or the shot discussed next – the reverse hit or reverse pull.

These variations illustrate how the reverse sweep has changed over the last half-decade, as more and more players use it and adapt it to their own requirements. And Dermott Reeve should take the credit for all of it. Apparently he is looking forward to the day a cricket book is published with a reverse sweep shown on the cover!

5. REVERSE HIT

As one of the quickest and most nimble international batsmen of his generation, Jonty Rhodes had the time to adjust his shots at the last minute. As a result, fans would often see him go down to reverse-sweep, only to jump into a more upright position as the ball bounced higher, and pull the ball away 'left-handed'. Such was his timing and strength that many of these 'reverse pulls' carried for six over gully – or 'short fine leg' as it became.

When to play the reverse hit

This depends largely on the field placing, and the lengths and lines the spinners are trying to bowl; but essentially you're playing the shot to break the shackles after a few maiden overs or dot balls; and above all, you're trying to upset the bowler's rhythm.

As a disruptive weapon, it is almost unparalleled. When Dermott Reeve first used the shot against Ravi Shastri in a match between Warwickshire and Glamorgan, fetching a ball from the rough outside his leg stump and smashing it out of Edgbaston, the Indian all-rounder was so shocked, he complained to the umpire that Reeve was batting left-handed. Shastri's composure in tatters, he soon became expensive and was taken off. Warwickshire won the match. Similarly, Brian McMillan used the shot to lift Muttiah Muralitharan out of Nairobi's cricket ground, a move that upset the Sri Lankan spinner's rhythm considerably.

Playing the reverse hit

As the ball is released, the back foot moves forward and just inside the line of the ball. The hands are reversed (as in hitting a reverse stick cross in hockey). Then bend your knees, and emulate the position of a backhand shot in squash. Swing through the ball with a hard follow-through: the power in the shot can be awesome.

The Rhodes version

Jonty Rhodes' version of Reeve's reverse hit resulted in some serious damage to bowling figures. His variation was similar in all respects to Reeve's, but instead of changing feet and turning hand over hand, he simply jumped into a square-on position, and played a 'squash backhand'. If you would like to learn to play this stroke, remember to keep your knees flexed to adjust to the height of the ball after it has bounced.

Practising the shot

The first thing to stress is this: if you've decided to learn to play the reverse hit, then you can't practise it enough.

The best ways of grooving this shot in your repertoire are progressive training and repetition. Remember, it is a shot that takes flair and confidence, and if you get it wrong, don't expect many sympathetic voices in the dressing room.

WRAPPING IT UP

This book covers all the cricket shots you are ever likely to play. Of course, there is much more to playing the game (and playing it well) than simply learning this 'vocabulary' of shots.

But now you have the basics – defensive and attacking shots, straight- and cross-batted shots, as well as the stances, guards and grips from which to launch your own match-winning performances – or simply survive.

Of course, it is no use poring over the instructions given here and studying the photographs unless you go out with bat and ball and practise each part of each shot over and over and over again. Each movement must be correctly practised, with careful attention paid to each part of the body. Slowly, the pieces will start to come together into the makings of a confident and correctly played shot. Focus on grooving just a few shots at first, and making these the cornerstone of your batting before going on to master, say, the hook shot or the reverse sweep.

The role you play in your team will also determine your focus. If you are the team's strike bowler, unless you are a genuine all-rounder, your focus should be on defensive shots and tactics, and on honing one or two run-making shots that will enable you to scramble a single and give the strike to the (hopefully) more recognized batsman at the other end. Likewise, if you open the batting for your team, you will have to have excellent defensive skills, but also the ability to cope with short-pitched and vicious bowling. Middle-order batters should have a range of shots for playing spinners.

But technique is only half the battle; as you begin to string your shots together into a carefully judged and useful innings, other qualities will come into play: mental strength, focus, physical fitness, experience, strategy (i.e., the ability to assess each stage of the game and respond appropriately in tactical terms), knowledge of the pitch and conditions, team skills, and so on. Even something as apparently minor as what you drink in the breaks in the game can have an impact on your batting. This is the allure, the special magic of cricket – no matter how gifted an athlete or technically brilliant a batter you are, there are always a dozen variables to contend with – or to use to your advantage.

BRADMAN'S UNRECOGNIZED LEGACY: HIS 'ROTARY' BATTING METHOD

Is it possible for one man to be correct but to have been ignored? This is the question that Lancashire county cricketer Tony Shillinglaw poses in his 2003 book *Bradman Revisited: The Legacy of Sir Donald Bradman*. (Shillinglaw played cricket at the Birkenhead Park Cricket Club, the same club for which Tim Noakes's father played in the 1930s, one of those remarkable coincidences that keep cropping up in cricket lore.)

Shillinglaw's hypothesis is that Sir Donald Bradman was the greatest cricketer of all time not because of some biological advantage that was never identified in his lifetime, but because the solo cricket games he invented and practised in his backyard during his boyhood in the small South Australian village of Bowral produced an almost unique batting method. Yet because this method of Bradman's conflicted with the batting orthodoxy that began to be taught after the Second World War – especially through the influence of the MCC coaching manual within the Commonwealth nations – it became convenient to label Bradman as a 'one-off genius' whose unorthodox method could and should not be adopted by those who lacked Bradman's allegedly uniquely superior biological attributes. What worked for Bradman, so the story goes, cannot possibly work for any other player, now or in the future.

And there the debate might have rested, if not for Shillinglaw's persistent worry that perhaps the legacy of the Don's genius was going to waste. This despite the fact that Bradman's book on cricket, *The Art of Cricket*, is considered to be the 'bible' of cricket coaching – in the words of another legendary Australian player, Richie Benaud, it is the 'most brilliant coaching book ever written and illustrated'. Yet nowhere in his book does Bradman suggest that his batting method was unique, much less a superior solution to the challenges faced by batsmen; nor does he clearly identify what differentiated his method from that taught in the MCC coaching manual.

Indeed, only the most eagle-eyed reader would detect that Bradman's batting style was fundamentally different from the traditional one. It is a measure of the man's humility that when Bradman's 'secret' was presented to him by Shillinglaw shortly before his death, his only comment was: 'I have read Tony's [Shillinglaw's] words with interest and some embarrassment because I lay no claim to the expertise with which he credits me.'

In his book, Shillinglaw builds his case that this 'secret' of Bradman's was the development of what indeed might be the ideal batting method. He assembles his arguments according to the following facts.

Donald Bradman was never coached. Even more interesting, he had never even witnessed a first-class cricket match until he found himself playing first-class cricket for New South Wales. And he did not read books on cricket by other well-known players. Up till the age of seventeen, he played almost no formal cricket. By then, the method he had devised was uniquely his own. And unlike many young players who found that unorthodox techniques worked for them at the beginning of their playing careers, Bradman never found it necessary to change his method as he rose up through the ranks of the game.

Despite never having been coached, Bradman's rise in cricket was meteoric. He played his first cricket match when he was eleven years old on a dirt pitch at his junior school in Bowral, South Australia. He scored 55 not out. During the remainder of his school years, he played two more matches on a concrete pitch covered with coir matting. He scored 115 and 72 in those matches, both times not out. So in the only three competitive matches he played during his entire school career, Bradman scored 242 runs without losing his wicket.

At thirteen, Bradman played two matches for the Bowral senior team, scoring 37 and 29 – once again without losing his wicket. By the time he left school at age fourteen, he had played in all of five matches and had never even practised on a grass pitch. Yet he had scored 308 runs without once being dismissed.

Bradman's serious cricket career began three years later when he became a regular member of the Bowral first team at the start of the 1925/26 cricket season. In the interim, he had played three more matches, bringing his grand total of completed innings to eight. Yet he completed the season by scoring 1 318 runs at an average of 101,3 – including a District record score of 300, and another of 234 not out against a team that included the gifted leg-spinner Bill O'Reilly, whom Bradman would later name as the greatest bowler of all time. Of that innings, O'Reilly would later write: 'I could not assimilate the knowledge that a pocket-sized schoolboy could give me such a complete lacing.'

This astonishing sequence led Shillinglaw to ask the question: 'What led a seventeen-year-old, who up until then, was the scorer of only 375 runs in his life, into having the capacity to immediately reach such a peak and go on to produce the phenomenal batting record the cricketing world is now familiar with, without ever having a significant lapse in form at any level he played?' Given that Bradman never adapted his technique, a style that was set before he ever played a first-class match, his unique batting methods warranted closer scrutiny.

Bradman taught himself not how to play cricket, but how to control a fast-moving ball, a crucial distinction. This principle informed his own coaching approach: 'Coaching should deal with what to do with the ball, not so much as how to do it. The coach must have sufficient intelligence not to be dogmatic but to discern what method is best for the pupil.' Hitting rather than thinking about how to hit is perhaps best understood in terms of the evolution of the human brain. We evolved the archaic brain pathways necessary to control complex movements – the 'what to do with the ball' components – long before we developed the pathways to analyse *how* we do it. Evolution has thus provided us with all the brain pathways necessary to bowl, catch and hit the cricket ball without engaging the higher brain centres that control thinking – and which evolved only much later. Moreover, these archaic brain pathways are best developed by incessant practice.

The training method that Bradman evolved arose as a game to keep him occupied after school. This game, which determined the batting method he developed, was dependent on the exact dimensions of the backyard of his parent's home in Bowral. Bradman himself described it thus: 'At the back of our home was an 800-gallon water tank set on a round brick stand. From the tank to the laundry door was a distance of about eight feet [close to three metres]. The area underfoot was cemented and, with all doors shut, this portion was enclosed on three sides and roofed over so that I could play there on wet days. Armed with a small cricket stump (which I used as a bat) I would throw a golf ball at this brick stand and try to hit the ball on the rebound. The golf ball came back at great speed and to hit it at all with the round stump was no easy task.'

This became an intricate game, in which the young boy worked out how wickets would be lost and boundaries scored. Using this system, he played 'Test matches' in which he batted for all the players on both sides.

With hindsight, Bradman conceded, 'This rather extraordinary and primitive idea was purely a matter of amusement, but looking back over the years I can understand how it must have developed the co-ordination of brain, eye and muscle which was to serve me so well in important matches later on.'

Bradman also taught himself to field almost by accident, developing 'another form of amusement' in which he threw a cricket or golf ball at a low pole fence, with rounded poles lying horizontally. Only if the ball struck the poles at a certain angle would it return to him at a catchable height: 'Obviously this also developed the ability to throw accurately, because if I missed the selected spot, it would mean a walk to retrieve the ball.' Perhaps as a result of the skills that he developed in this fielding game, Bradman became one of the best fielders of his day and one of the most accurate throwers from close distance.

Bradman developed an unorthodox method of batting as a result of this self-training. In particular, his grip was unusual. The face of his bat was closed and the tip of the bat rested between his feet, touching his left toe (see p. 31). This contrasts with the more usual method in which the bat face is more open, parallel to the crease, facing the bowler (see p. 30). Since Bradman's bat faced towards mid-wicket rather than directly up the pitch, so his grip rotated further round (clockwise) towards the back of the bat when viewed from above. As he described: 'Notice that the inverted V formed by the thumb and first finger of the right hand is straight in line with the insertion of the handle down the back of the blade.' In this position, his grip is rotated about 90° clockwise (backwards, when looking from above) and sometimes even further from the more traditional grip.

Nevertheless, in his cricketing 'bible', Bradman fails to emphasize how radically his grip differs from that which is conventionally taught. He evades the debate by stating: 'I refuse to be dogmatic about one's grip, because I believe various holds can be satisfactory. So much depends on the batsman's methods.... I refuse to condemn an unorthodox grip just because it is different. The use of wrist and arms and the method of stroke production cannot be stereotyped.'

Elsewhere, he wrote, 'I am more inclined to teach boys what to do than how to do it – so long as there is no fundamental or glaring error. Better to hit the ball with an apparently unorthodox style than to miss it with a correct one.'

Of course, here he could be describing himself – he was the most successful striker of the ball in the history of cricket. Yet before he established himself internationally, he was considered not only unorthodox, but an 'ugly, half-cock player', in the words of one commentator. Another wrote of the young Bradman, '[He] was one of the most curious mixtures of good and bad batting that I have ever seen… He will always be in the category of the brilliant but unsound ones…. He does not correct mistakes or look as if he were trying to do so.'

An uncritical reader of Bradman's *The Art of Cricket*, who had never seen Bradman bat, could be forgiven if he or she failed to appreciate just how different

Bradman's stance and grip and his initial movements were compared to what has been taught for the last 50 years. Of course, it was because Bradman's batting technique was so unorthodox that he had to grip the bat differently.

Bradman argued only that the position of his left hand produced what in golfing terms is known as a 'slightly shut' face, the benefit of which is that it keeps the ball on the ground, especially when playing on-side strokes. In other words, the further forward (nearer to the plane of the bat face) the left (top) hand holds the bat, the more likely it is that the ball will be struck in the air when playing shots on the on side. Indeed, Bradman was meticulous in keeping the ball down when playing cross-batted shots on the on side, aiming to hit the ball almost directly to the ground when he played the hook and pull shots.

Bradman was not blind to criticism or closed to experimentation, writing: 'I experimented, worked out the pros and cons and eventually decided not to change my natural grip.'

But the more radical component of Bradman's method was that **the initial movement of his bat during the backlift was towards second slip and not directly backwards towards the wicket** – as prescribed by the original MCC coaching manual. Greg Chappell, considered by many to be the second greatest Australian batsman after Bradman, observed that Bradman achieved this initial movement merely by cocking his wrists with his forearm muscles, without any movement of his shoulders and upper arms. The value of this is that it minimizes weight redistribution resulting from this initial movement.

Bradman was clearly conscious of the unorthodoxy of this method, and defended it as follows:

> Reams of matter have been written about the necessity of taking one's bat back perfectly straight. Some coaching books even advocate taking the bat back towards the stumps. Well now, this is the sort of illustration which proves the need for intelligent coaching as distinct from strict rule of thumb.
>
> Don't let me be misunderstood. I am all in favour of a straight bat at the right time and place, but technique must be the servant, not the master.
>
> Too many players fail because their thoughts are concentrated on where their left elbow is or where something else is, instead of on hitting the ball.
>
> I was never conscious of my backlift and I did not take any particular notice where the bat went until I saw movie shots of me in action. Then it was clear my initial bat movement almost invariably was towards the slips.

This was accentuated by my grip and stance and perhaps it should have been straighter, but to me, anyway, the important thing was where the bat went on the downswing.

For defensive shots the bat should naturally be as straight as possible, but for a pull shot, for instance, a perfectly straight backlift would make it far harder to execute the stroke.

The basic technique of a straight bat is sound for defence but there should be all possible emphasis on attack, on the aggressive outlook. Think of some of the great batsmen and you will find very few who did not depart in some degree from orthodoxy.

Bradman considered that the key to correct batting was to be in the correct position at the top of the backlift, a position he reached shortly after ball release and at the exact time when he would be tracking the ball during the first 120 milliseconds of its flight, calculating, in his subconscious mind, not just where the ball would pitch but more probably exactly where in its flight he would strike it. But in *The Art of Cricket*, Bradman does not explain exactly what that position is. Instead, he offered the opinion: 'If we could take moving pictures of all leading batsmen in action, particularly when they were not conscious that a camera was focused on them, I think we would find the majority of them take the blade rather more towards first or second slip. That initial movement probably allows a flexibility which the strictly orthodox does not.'

Here the term 'probably' is a measure of Bradman's reluctance to force his ideas on others. There is no doubt, however, that he was convinced that the conventional method made it much more difficult to play cross-batted shots towards leg. So perhaps his modesty has not served the game well. However, in a letter to Shillinglaw written near the end of his life, Bradman wrote more forcefully: 'The perpendicular bat theory virtually eliminates pull shots (which can only be played with a cross bat) and square cuts (except by angling the blade) which, in turn, is a recipe for giving catches in the slips.'

Also revealing is Bradman's suggestion that the batsman whose backlift might point towards the slips would have to be filmed unawares. The inference is that if he knew he was being observed or recorded, he would revert to what he had been taught and hence considered to be correct. This suggests the damning power of the accusation of 'unorthodoxy', an accusation that has exercised a peculiar hold over the game for decades.

Shillinglaw draws a parallel to the career of Wally Hammond, a contemporary of Bradman's, who was at times considered his batting equal. Responding to the statement that he would never play for England because he was too 'unorthodox', in particular because he played with a bat that was not vertical, Hammond modified his game to restrict his leg-side cross-batted shots. This might explain why his Test match batting average, acquired in a career that overlapped with Bradman's (1928–1948) was 58,45 – compared to Bradman's 99,94.

In an introduction to the re-release of his 1934 coaching film, Bradman stated that the standards of fielding had increased substantially since his era, but he was silent, perhaps intentionally, on the current state of batting and bowling compared to his day. However, he did note that 'In batting, there are very many competent players but for some reason, maybe coaching, the emphasis seems now to be more on forward play. There are fewer batsmen who are predominantly back foot players. Hence we don't see as many cut shots and pull shots. One cause seems to be the tendency to use heavier bats. These are fine for the pendulum-type shots but militate against strokes across the line of flight.'

Bradman's initial motion was to move the bat and hence the centre of mass of the batter plus his cricket bat, away from the body towards point. Thus his weight was also transferred in the same direction, that is, onto the balls of his feet. In contrast, the 'orthodox' technique, in which the bat moves backward, initially transfers the weight onto the back foot from which it is extremely difficult to perform any shot other than one off the front foot. So to play backward requires a secondary movement that returns the weight to the balls of the feet. Perhaps one factor contributing to the dominance of front-foot play in world cricket is because of the weight transfer to the back foot resulting from a backlift that goes towards the stumps. Alec Bedser, the great English batsman, came close to the nub of the matter when he noted that Bradman's backlift and downswing created a 'flow' towards the ball – what today we might more scientifically describe as a rotary movement of the bat as it travelled along the continuum from backlift to downswing.

As a result of his unusual technique, Bradman was considered 'unorthodox'. In the words of Shillinglaw: 'His "genius" could be understood as a concept but it defied rational explanation. The accepted concept of orthodoxy could not be challenged by one man, no matter how outstanding.' Furthermore, since Bradman was unorthodox, it was considered inappropriate even to consider studying his 'ugly' method. Shillinglaw includes a 1933 correspondence that offers this gem: 'At the other end was Bradman. And if his partner shone in orthodoxy then the little champion positively sparkled in unorthodoxy. Balls that according to all the tenets of cricket should have been handled with a meticulously straight bat, were rudely dispatched boundary-wards with a blade that artistically flashed across the line of flight without recording the suggestion that the user thereof was indulging in the "cross-bat" so despised by the orthodox confreres of the willow... Never was the mastery of Bradman more exemplified than in that single off-theory over of Thompson's [sic] when every ball was cracked to the unprotected leg, while the covers presented the appearance of an over starched paddock of flannel-clad fieldsmen.'

One advantage of Bradman's technique was that it allowed balls pitched even far outside the off stumps to be pulled to leg. This presented those who bowled to Bradman with significant problems. South African bowlers in particular suffered from Bradman's batting onslaught. In five innings against the South Africans, Bradman scored 806 runs, once not out, for an average of 201,50 with four hundreds. It is perhaps not surprising, then, that the most detailed description of what it was like bowling to Bradman has been provided by the South African bowler A. J. Bell. The hapless Bell bowled to Bradman in seven matches, often for an entire day, without once claiming his wicket. Shillinglaw quotes from Bell's autobiography to highlight the difficulties bowlers faced in choosing the best line and length when bowling to Bradman:

One pitches a good length on his leg stump and the ball gathers another coat of paint off the pickets of the fine leg boundary.... If you bowl just short of a length on the off pin he takes great pains over his shot and is content to push it down the gully for a single, or just out of reach of the unfortunate fielder.... We tried for four and a half months to get him caught in the slips by bowling short just outside off stump. His wonderful placing and command over the ball made life absolutely untenable.... He seems to know what kind of ball you are going to bowl and where you are going to bowl it. He makes up his mind in a flash and does not hit the ball to the fielder as a great many do, but places it just out of reach and grins cheerfully.... His hook shot is incredible. He steps right back onto his wicket (one does not see much wicket when he is batting) and cracks the ball plumb in the middle of the bat.... When he does mistime the ball [rather, when his prediction of the exact trajectory and position of the ball was incorrect, as this is the more probable error – authors' insertion], *and this is very infrequently, the ball does not shoot up in the air... but drops harmlessly on the ground. This is due to the fact that every shot he plays, he intends the ball to hit the ground just a couple of yards from his feet. In all his shots he seems to turn the wrist over so that on the completion of the stroke the face of the bat is towards the ground.*

Bell also noticed that Bradman never attempted to score in front of the wicket when facing fast or medium bowlers who were fresh. Rather he 'glides the ball down the leg side or hits it like a bullet between point and third man'.

Bradman considered adopting other techniques but found these limited his run-scoring ability: 'I allowed my bat to rest on the ground between my feet simply because it was a comfortable and natural position. It is regarded as more orthodox to teach a pupil to rest his bat behind his right toe. This position encourages a straighter backlift, is perhaps sounder for defensive play, but I feel it has greater limitations in versatile stroke making.'

Shillinglaw concludes that the recognized 'orthodoxy' is based on a pendulum motion of the bat in which the batter's first priority is defence of the wicket, whereas Bradman's focus was on attacking the bowler and dictating terms to him. It is the latter approach that seems to have been adopted by the current generation of exceptional Australian batsmen.

Why has orthodoxy survived in the modern coaching manuals whereas no mention is made of Bradman's technique and how it fails to conform to this orthodoxy? Shillinglaw notes that it has been much easier to dismiss Bradman as a 'one-off' than to challenge the orthodoxy. Nevertheless, he feels it is imperative that we investigate why one individual was able to have a test average 30% better than the next best average in the history of the game. Biological factors alone cannot explain this significant a difference – they do not differ by 30% between the very best and the next best human in any particular activity.

In fact, a fundamental teaching in science is that it is dangerous to presume a cause unless it has been proven. Since we have no evidence that Bradman was biologically superior, we must entertain the possibility that Bradman's brilliance might have been the result of his superior and unorthodox batting technique.

Shillinglaw concludes: 'Bradman appeared to select every stroke and continue its motion from the same advanced position of perfect balance.' The advantage of this has to be obvious. Once his subconscious had selected the type of shot to be played, the forward swing of his bat could be adjusted to accommodate either a defensive shot with a straight bat or an attacking shot with a cross-bat. There was no need to produce a different sequence, depending on the nature of the delivery. For example, to hit a pull shot from a straight backlift requires the bat to move laterally away from the ball before it can begin to move towards the ball. No such limitation exists in the Bradman method, where the swing of the bat can rotate according to the dictates of the ball.

WHAT THE CAMERA REVEALS

Further evidence of this is provided by extensive analysis of film footage of Bradman, including his coaching video. What is of significant interest is that he played shots in Test matches that were not repeated in his coaching video. Typically, these were cross-bat shots off the back foot to all parts of the field. These are not listed among the 'orthodox' batting shots included either in his video or in his book on coaching.

His stance and grip, as discussed above, were unorthodox. Nevertheless, his head and body were absolutely still at the time of ball release. The only observable movement immediately before ball release was the beginning of his backlift. At the moment of ball release, the tip of his bat had reached the level of the top of the stumps.

His backlift was achieved by cocking his wrists without moving his upper arms or shoulders and was directed towards second slip/point. This enabled the transfer of weight to the balls of his feet, not onto his back foot. As a result, he was able to move onto either the back or front foot to play his strokes. However, he preferred to play back, except when the ball was extremely full, or he was stepping out of his crease to attack a spin bowler.

The direction of his backlift allowed Bradman to achieve a constant, repeatable 'set' position from which he could execute all his straight- and cross-batted shots. In the case of a straight-batted shot (a drive to the off side, for example), his bat would return to the line of the stumps as it came forward. As a result, by the time it struck the ball, the blade of the bat was straight and headed in the direction in which the ball was to be driven. This technique, in which the bat rotated through a circle in the course of the backlift and forward stroke, has been termed Bradman's 'rotary' method by Shillinglaw. Our most recent analysis shows that, without exception, all the great batsmen of the past – including W.G. Grace, Graeme Pollock, Garfield Sobers, Viv Richards and Brian Lara – all followed this technique, as do all the current batsmen in the all-conquering Australian team of 2007.

In contrast, if the ball was short enough to pull or hook, Bradman's backlift would continue until it was above the level of his shoulder. From there the bat would travel directly to the point where it would strike the ball. As the bat was travelling on a downward path, the ball would be struck towards the ground. By rolling his wrists, Bradman made doubly certain that he did not hit the ball into the air.

Finally, when driving on the front foot, Bradman rotated his upper body and struck the ball as if he was playing a golf shot, a phenomenon seen in many modern players who are powerful strikers of the cricket ball – most notably the Australians Matthew Hayden and Adam Gilchrist.

Indeed, our unpublished study of eight of the current top batsmen in world cricket in 2006 (including Ricky Ponting, Jacques Kallis, Mohammad Yousuf, Inzamam-ul-Haq, Kevin Pietersen, Damien Martin, Herschelle Gibbs and Andrew Symonds) reveals that none lifts his bat directly backwards at the start of his backswing. Indeed it is difficult now to find a leading Australian batsman who does not lift his bat towards the slips, suggesting that finally in his own country, the legacy of Bradman is being honoured not just in memory, but in the practice of the sport he dominated.

Shillinglaw proposes that formally recognizing, accepting and adopting the 'rotary' batting style would provide the true and lasting legacy of Sir Donald Bradman as his gift to the game of cricket.

IF BRADMAN IS CORRECT, WHAT DOES THIS MEAN FOR THE COACHING OF YOUNG CRICKETERS?

1. **Learning to control a fast-moving ball must be the first requirement.**
   If Bradman's brilliance resulted from the hundreds of hours that he spent playing his boyhood cricket matches, then perhaps young children should be encouraged to learn cricket first by hitting a tennis ball against a wall with a cricket bat. Then they should graduate to using a golf ball and a cricket stump. Once they have mastered that technique (as Bradman did), they can begin to learn the nuances of cricket. Interestingly, Bjorn Börg, five times Wimbledon champion by the age of 24, has said that he learned to play tennis by hitting the ball against the wall for hours each day. To win a 'point', he had to return the ball ten times.

2. **One reason why orthodoxy and over-coaching fail might be because they do not develop the art of controlling the fast-moving cricket ball at the right age as effectively as a simple game (like those Bradman invented) does.**
   There is now considerable evidence that there are key periods when the brain 'learns' certain skills. If there is no exposure to that skill during

that key period of brain development, then that skill will never be properly mastered. For example, the ability to play a specific musical instrument probably requires that the child be exposed to these activities from a very young age. Similarly, the fact that Bradman spent most of his childhood playing his imaginary cricket matches suggests that the optimum period to develop these skills is probably from the age of seven onwards – perhaps even younger.

3. **Shillinglaw strongly believes that 'the very minute a young player is told to stand with his bat open-faced behind his rear foot, the battle is lost. From this position the only natural movement is straight back. Bradman's style of batting cannot be adopted from this stance.'**
This opinion needs to be seriously considered by future generations of cricket coaches.

4. **Bradman's ultimate secret was that his technique allowed him to play a wider range of strokes than are usually described in classic cricket texts.**
His less conventional strokes (which looked more like golf or tennis shots) are becoming increasingly common in the repertoires of twenty-twenty and one-day batting maestros such as Matthew Hayden, Andrew Symonds, Yousuf Khan, V.V.S. Laxman and others.

POSTSCRIPT: BOWLING TO THE DON

Perhaps the final word belongs to the man reputed to be the fastest bowler in history, Australian Jeff Thomson, in an interview with television personality and cricket lover, Michael Parkinson. Thomson remembered Bradman, then in his late sixties, attending the opening of a new cricket field. Two aspiring cricketers, on the verge of selection to the state team, had asked if they could bowl to him, and the old warrior agreed.

At first 'the young men bowled respectfully at him, aware both of his age and the fact that he had neither pads nor gloves. But when Bradman started playing shots, they quickened up and eventually were bowling flat out... the quicker they bowled, the harder Bradman smote them to the boundary. It was bloody magnificent. All my life I had looked at his record and thought – how can anyone be twice as good as Greg Chappell? That day I found out.'

VISION AND BATTING

'The brain is a better cricketer than you'll ever be.'

Greg Chappell, *Cricket: The Making of Champions*

While technique and tactics have been central to cricket manuals for over a century, the physiology of the game is relatively new in the popular consciousness of the game. Even today's increasingly sophisticated players and audiences, who have a layperson's knowledge of stress fractures and rotator cuffs and bone spurs (all Greek to players and fans of a generation ago), nevertheless still refer to the 'Magic Spray' that comes out when a player gets a nasty knock, a name that only half hides in humour the rather superstitious relationship the public has with sports medicine.

Still, physiology has entered the public debate, and will stay there: from the media to the stands, discussions abound over players being over-bowled, backs that won't stand the strain of particular actions, shoulder and wrist movements that will help or hinder the run-scoring ability of the latest up-and-coming international star, and so on.

It would seem, then, that cricket manuals and popular discourse have finally caught up with the game's development: that we are now discussing everything that needs to be discussed. But this is not so.

One crucial – perhaps even fundamental – physiological aspect still needs to be understood and incorporated into the teaching and playing of the game: vision.

PREDICTING THE PATH OF THE BALL

Bowlers should be taught how to disguise critical cues, present false clues, increase the number of possible relevant clues, vary all the dimensions of speed, swing, flight and direction, and finally provide the critical clues as late as possible (Stretch and Bartlett, 2000).

More than almost any other human activity, sport illustrates the ruthless Darwinian process of selection. Those without the necessary skills fail to advance to the next level of competition, and remain at the level at which they are competent. Those who have the necessary aptitudes, whether physiological or psychological, advance.

There are many selective factors that will determine the level to which a cricketer can advance: concentration, desire, courage, application, fitness and so on. But the most obvious, at least for batters, are the dual but different abilities of their subconscious brains to process information quickly enough to deal with incoming fast deliveries, and precisely enough to play the deceptive flights and spins produced by slow bowlers.

Without these capabilities, often simplistically labelled 'hand-eye co-ordination', a batter will never reach the highest levels of sport. This is the law of the sporting jungle, and it applies across the board. The reason that some international batsmen have a batting average in the 30s while others average in the 60s may well hinge on these subconscious mental abilities – the ability of expert batters to see clues in the bowler's run-up and delivery action, and to predict the future path of the ball with an accuracy that defies understanding, simply by tracking the first few metres of each delivery's flight. Batting will always be easier for those who can subconsciously select the relevant visual information and process it more quickly, thereby having more time to choose the most appropriate shot and execute it with exquisite precision.

But the great irony that this chapter will explore is that ultimately, the batter must hit the ball *without knowing exactly where it is*, nor indeed precisely when it will be there. Similarly the close-in fielder must catch the ball without knowing exactly where it is, nor the exact moment that it will arrive in his grasp.

In other words, successful batting and consistent catching are, at the moment of impact, based almost entirely on blind assumption; yet most top players make this predictive leap with an accuracy of timing and position that cannot be equalled by any human-made system.

To review the raw split-second data of what actually happens (in terms of vision and decision-making) when batters execute a shot is to wonder how any batsman survives more than one delivery. Using information gleaned in the first third of each delivery's flight, he must predict the moment at which the ball will reach him with an accuracy of 2–4 milliseconds, and with a future positional accuracy in three-dimensional space of 1–2 centimetres in any direction. In other words, he needs to know *exactly* when and where the ball will arrive to be played. As predictions of the future go, these are extraordinarily specific: the tiniest error in predicting either the future arrival time of the delivery, or its exact position at that instant, or indeed the correct movement of the bat, will usually result in dismissal.

The great irony is that ultimately, the batter must hit the ball without knowing exactly where it is, nor precisely when it will be there.

And yet at the highest levels of the game, batsmen make correct decisions, and almost perfect predictions, for dozens, if not hundreds of consecutive deliveries. This is largely because they have removed one of the unknown factors from their unconscious calculation processes: their own movements. As seasoned international players, their technique and the biomechanics of their batting are grooved and practised to such a degree that they know exactly how they will respond to certain deliveries. But the need to predict, to launch a stroke at a point in space without being certain that the ball will ever arrive in that point at the right time, cannot be removed by practice, and it remains the greatest threat to top players. It is the errors in their predictions, often caused by misreading and misunderstanding their visual senses, which lead to their dismissals.

However, this is not simply a struggle between a batsman and a point in space in which the ball may or may not show up: there is an agent provocateur at work here! If batters are trying to gain the clearest and most accurate visual sense of the future position of the ball, then bowlers are equally determined to obscure that sense. In fact, a good bowler is one who is able to produce deceptive visual information during his approach and delivery, misleading signals that will persuade the batter to play a stroke where the ball mysteriously is not. As an American baseball pitcher said: 'Hitting is timing; pitching is upsetting timing.' Exactly the same principles apply to batting and bowling. Batting is timing; bowling is upsetting timing.

In this way, cricket has evolved 'to produce a balanced contest between the visual-motor skills of the batsman and the strength and skills of the bowler. Batting is possible (or batsmen would refuse to play), but not all the time (or bowlers would refuse to play). The abilities of the best batsman against the fastest bowlers reveal the limits of the (human) visual-motor system' (Land and McLeod, 2000).

Those limits, and their breaking-points, have become cricketing lore – think of Harold Larwood shocking Australian cricket into the twentieth century in the 1932/33 Bodyline series, Jeff Thomson eliciting a boycott by the Indian team in 1977/78, and Curtly Ambrose annihilating England with figures of 8 for 40, with the rest of the team retired hurt, at Port of Spain in 1994.

But how do great batters continue to achieve with some consistency what might appear to be impossible? And how do the most skilled bowlers exploit the natural limits of the human visual-motor system to their best advantage?

THE VISUAL CHALLENGE POSED BY FAST BOWLING

In the early 1980s, Tim Noakes and his colleagues at the University of Cape Town wanted to establish whether batters differed in their ability to process early information about the delivery in order to make accurate choices about which stroke to play.

They enlisted the help of former South African Test player Peter Kirsten, a batsman widely recognized as one of the best players of pace bowling in his generation. However, they soon discovered that even Kirsten was unable to hit the ball when it was delivered by a bowling machine at speeds in excess of 130km per hour. Yet out in the middle, Kirsten had comfortably dealt with deliveries travelling in excess of 150km per hour. This simple experiment proved that an expert batsman needs to observe the bowler's run-up and delivery if his brain is to compute the delivery's future trajectory when travelling at speeds of more than 130km per hour. In other words, the batter relies heavily on a kind of visual early warning system, here referred to as advance cues, during the bowler's approach and delivery. Without these cues, he becomes increasingly less able to face genuine pace with any degree of confidence.

The switch of the indoor lighting was then linked to the bowling machine Kirsten was facing, so that the lights were turned off at the moment the ball left the bowling machine. The results were telling: even if he had sight of the ball for as little as the first 100–200 milliseconds before the light faded (of the approximately 550 milliseconds of the ball's flight), Kirsten – and presumably a player of his class – could predict the trajectory and exactly where it would pitch with 70% accuracy.

Lesser batsmen, however, were less successful, and less inclined to wait around to see if their predictions had been correct: some provincial bowlers asked to bat in these testing conditions simply ran from the wicket as soon as the lights died down.

On the basis of these results, the researchers drew the simple conclusion: a superior ability to predict the ball's trajectory early in its flight is probably a genetic gift innate in all 'natural' batsmen, and is simply developed to an exceptional degree in cricketing geniuses such as Sir Donald Bradman, Sir Garfield Sobers, Graeme Pollock, Barry Richards, Brian Lara and Sachin Tendulkar. This was not a novel suggestion. Bill Ponsford, who batted with Bradman in the 1930s, said, 'Don sees the ball two yards earlier than the rest of us' (Fingleton, 1946). Similarly, Garry Sobers described early detection as central to his success: 'I was never coached. I had a simple approach, based on the theory that if a batsman picked up the ball early enough, he could position himself to play whatever shot he thought the ball deserved' (1996, p. 78).

However, the Kirsten experiment revealed that even a world-class batsman needed substantial visual information for shot selection: even though he could predict the trajectory of the delivery with just 100–200 milliseconds worth of information (before the lights went out), and even though his predictions of line and length were remarkably accurate, the best he could manage in response to the delivery was a

'Don sees the ball two yards earlier than the rest of us.'

– Bill Ponsford on Donald Bradman

defensive parry. He had simply not received enough information to be able to make a confident enough prediction about the ball's position relative to him to commit to an attacking stroke.

The conclusion drawn from this experiment is that Kirsten needed to see more than just the first quarter of the delivery's flight if he was to judge its final position and time of arrival with sufficient precision to play an attacking shot.

DEFENDING IN THE DARK

Why could Kirsten play a defensive stroke but not an attacking one? The answer lies in his straight bat. When you are defending with a vertical blade, you don't need to predict the final position of the ball on the vertical plane with any accuracy: whether it hits your bat 1cm or 40cm off the pitch, it is still a safe shot. Nor is timing important, since the ball is meeting you, rather than you meeting it.

ADVANCE CLUES: THE BATTER'S EARLY WARNING SYSTEM

The explanation for Kirsten's dilemma – his inability to play an attacking shot to deliveries travelling at more than 130km per hour – was the absence of advance cues in the experiment. An impassive, immobile bowling machine reveals little about the nature of the delivery it is going to produce: an increase in the pitch of its motor might suggest a quicker ball, and the point on the pitch at which it seems to be aimed should give some clues about the length of the delivery; but even these were removed from the scenario in the author's experiment, as batsmen were given earplugs and the machine was hidden behind a sheet, the ball appearing through a specially cut hole.

In other words, batsmen who participated in the experiment found themselves starved of the advance cues they were used to in match conditions. As already stated, the bowler is trying to deceive the batsman into a false shot. Like a poker player, he is trying to make the batter read his intentions incorrectly. But like so many poker players, he is simultaneously betraying a wealth of information through tiny subconscious signals, most of which he doesn't know he is broadcasting.

The following are just some of the ways in which he is telegraphing his intentions as he kicks off from his mark:

- **The speed of his run-up** – the faster the approach, the faster, or shorter, the delivery might be.
- **The point of delivery with regard to the popping crease** – tight against the stumps, and it might be a slower ball fishing for an LBW appeal, or an outswinger. Wider of the stumps, perhaps a fast yorker speared in at middle stump.
- **His grip** – the ball deeper in his fingers suggests a slower delivery.

- **The angle of the seam and shiny side of the ball** – most international bowlers try to hide this information from the batsmen, sometimes by cocking their wrist down over the ball until the point of release, or by holding their other hand over it, as mastered by India's Javagal Srinath and Pakistan's Wasim Akram.
- **The speed of the arm movement prior to and at the moment of releasing the ball.**
- **The exact position in space and the precise moment at which the ball is released** – in quick bowlers, a fractionally later release signals a short ball. Spinners who are looking to give the ball plenty of air to generate more drift and bounce might release it fractionally early.
- **The action of the wrist at the moment of release** – a wrist snapped straight down can signal a bouncer, while a quick snap down to the left or right, or a pushing action, can indicate an outswinger or inswinger, or a cutter. The position of the wrist is also critical to reading leg-spinners.
- **The position of the front shoulder at the moment of delivery** – a dropped front shoulder almost always signals a short ball.

It seems that batters use advance cues predominantly to predict length. Thus, having bet his wicket and his innings on a particular length, he then makes his initial movement either back or forwards.

BREAKDOWN OF THE BATTER'S RESPONSE TO A DELIVERY

As the bowler runs in, the batsman begins his search for anticipatory cues that will allow the earliest possible detection of the future flight pattern and velocity of the delivery. As stated above, the clues he is most urgently seeking are those that will hint at a possible length, to reveal whether his initial movement must be forward or back. It is probably that the very best batsmen in the world have already predicted the length of the delivery (with considerable accuracy) by the time the ball is released.

A striking example is that of Brian Lara, who was asked whether he had been nervous at the point in his innings when he had equalled – but not yet beaten – Sir Garfield Sobers' world record score of 365, when batting against England in Antigua in 1994. He conceded that he had been anxious for the first two deliveries (dot balls). But, he said, as bowler Chris Lewis ran in for the third delivery, he lost his anxiety: he knew during Lewis's approach to the wicket that the delivery would be short. In fact, Lara was in position so early for the hook shot that took him to the new world record, he almost stood on his stumps.

Once the ball has been released, the batter views it for as long as he needs to make a decision on the exact stroke he will play. This is known as the viewing time (VT).

Having decided which stroke to play, the batsman then experiences a latency time

(LT) during which his motor response to the delivery is organized and the necessary information travels via the various nervous pathways from his brain to his muscles. This latency time approximates what is known as the 'reaction time' and lasts about 180 milliseconds. Finally, the LT phase ends when the brain's commands finally reach the muscles, and initiate a response from those muscles that produce the batter's specific stroke. This is known as the movement time (MT).

THE DIFFERENCE BETWEEN GREAT AND GOOD

To the dependable amateur opening batsman, who faces the new ball every week for his club, this might all seem very removed from his experience of batting in the real world. After all, if one is talking about analysing batsmen's reactions to deliveries, then one is suggesting that all batsmen react in more or less the same way. And having faced the odd first-class or even retired Test bowler, our batsman is under no illusions about his own abilities: viewing times, latency times and such things are fine in theory, but he knows that there is simply no way that his reactions can be compared to anything even vaguely approaching those of a Bradman or a Sobers. Of course, he's quite wrong. The fact is that there is no evidence that superior batsmen have quicker reaction times or even superior visual skills. Rather, it is the way in which elite batters use the same information available to all batsmen that sets them apart.

Using a temporal occlusion study (one in which they allowed batters to see only part of the flight of the ball), Abernethy (1982) and Abernethy and Russell (1984) found that top batsmen can make accurate shot selections from shorter viewing times than less good batsmen. Furthermore, they suggested that more skilled batters are better at generating useful information from advance cues than less good batters.

The implications of the study were clear: the fundamental difference between elite batters and those with average skill is the ability of the elite to know where the ball is going even before it is delivered. England off-spinner Jim Laker confirmed this hypothesis when he said that 'Bradman seemed to know where the ball was going to pitch, what stroke he was going to play and how many runs he was going to score' (Williams, 1996). Greg Chappell, one of the great Australian batsmen to follow Bradman, has written: 'As the ball left the bowler's hand, all I saw was the ball and the bowler's hand. This gave me all the clues I needed to gauge the line, length and type of delivery' (2004, p. 146).

These authors also found that superior batsmen extracted more information from any equivalent viewing time and were therefore better able to cope with a reduced viewing time when facing a fast bowler. In contrast, when viewing times were reduced, less skilled batsmen were unable to respond appropriately – much as the weak batters ran away when the lights went out during the study in Cape Town.

In other words, batsmen succeed or fall by the wayside not because of their ocular and mental equipment, but because of how successfully or not they use that equipment. It is their brain 'software' that makes the difference, not their 'hardware'. Since these pioneering studies, a number of others have evaluated the use of visual information by batters. Penrose and Roach (1995) showed that skilled batsmen were significantly better than the less skilled at using advance cues to predict the subsequent line (radial variability) of bowling deliveries. They evaluated this by showing batsmen videos of different deliveries that ended 80 milliseconds before the bowler released the ball. This is known as the video-occlusion technique.

As more information was provided, less skilled batters increased their predictive ability, so that if more than the first 80 milliseconds of the delivery was shown, the predictive ability of the less-skilled batters was the same as that of the skilled batsmen. However, the longer decision time of the less-skilled batsmen left them with less time to take up a balanced position and to execute the appropriate cricket shot with the necessary control. The authors concluded that one of the keys to batting is the art of selective attention – the capacity to attend only to those crucial cues which predict the future line and length of the delivery, while ignoring the other cues that provide irrelevant information. They propose that batters learn to identify the most relevant advance and ball cues and concentrate exclusively on those clues, to the exclusion of all 'irrelevant' information.

More recently, in 2005 at the University of Cape Town, Sharhidd Taliep, Lester John and Tim Noakes, together with other researchers, measured the electrical activity of the brain in expert and novice batters while they watched video footage of inswing, outswing and slower deliveries. They found that the brains of expert batters needed about 10% less time (405 versus 445 milliseconds) to detect the outswing deliveries and about 12% less time (438 versus 495 milliseconds) to detect the inswing deliveries. In addition, expert batters had much greater alpha wave activity in the brain at the instant of ball release, indicating that they were more focused ('in the zone') at the moment the ball left the bowler's hand. This instant is what Greg Chappell calls the moment of 'fierce focus'. He notes that as a player, 'I used fierce focus for the shortest possible time because it required a lot of mental energy' (2004, p. 146).

The fundamental difference between elite batters and those with average skill is the ability of the elite to know where the ball is going even before it is delivered.

THE SACCADE HERESY

'Watch the ball!' It is a command as old as cricket, repeated mantra-like by coaches on five continents, and drummed into every child who has picked up a cricket bat. It has stood batters in good stead for almost 200 years, proving its worth on countless ovals, whether rustic cow pastures or Test venues packed to capacity. And it seems to have almost no foundation in reality.

The heretics were Land and McLeod in 2000. What they suggested went entirely contrary to traditional wisdom on vision: batsmen, they said, do *not* in fact watch the ball onto the bat. Using sophisticated video technology that recorded the direction of the batsman's gaze as well as his head movements, they observed batters facing a bowling machine. The results were revealing.

Batters kept their heads and eyes still for the first 140 milliseconds after the ball was released. Then they suddenly shifted their gaze downward by 7,5° in a rapid non-tracking movement known as a saccade, so that their eyes were looking at the spot on the pitch *where they expected the ball to pitch*.

The eyes then rotated upwards (relative to the head) for 300 milliseconds while the head moved downwards through the same angle, the eyes remaining fixed on the pitch where the ball was expected to bounce. Once the ball had bounced, the head and eyes quickly moved down in order to track the latter part of its flight. This occurred from about 350 to 550 milliseconds after the ball's release, after which the ball was no longer accurately tracked as the ball travelled progressively further 'ahead' of the batter's gaze. As a result, the eyes did not follow the ball for the last 100 milliseconds of the delivery.

How long had the batter watched the ball? 140 milliseconds after release; another 200 milliseconds after the ball had bounced: a total tracking time of around 340 milliseconds. And yet the delivery took 650 milliseconds to reach him. The numbers defied the coaches' mantra. The batter had had his eye on the ball for just 52% of its flight.

Did any batsmen watch the ball onto the bat? Certainly, the fuller the ball, the longer batsmen observed it before the first saccade. But a full, uninterrupted sight of the ball, with no saccade, happened only when the best batsman in the test group received a full toss. However, this did not imply that better batsmen did not need to make saccades. On the contrary, the study showed that when playing normal, bouncing deliveries, this batsman made his initial saccade earlier than the less gifted players.

Naturally, laboratory conditions can create artificial circumstances: the visual performance of these batters was studied for a relatively short time, and it is possible that the tracking patterns might have changed as they played themselves in. Perhaps, after an hour or two of batting, the batters might have been seeing the ball 'as big a football', and tracking deliveries for a greater proportion of their flight.

Nevertheless, the evidence suggests that batsmen do not watch the ball all the way onto the bat, no matter what seasoned veterans might claim. But is this a reason to scrap 150 years of coaching dogma? Should coaches start urging their young players to 'saccade after 140 milliseconds'? Of course not. Even if batters are not literally watching the ball all the way onto the bat, they should still be trained to try.

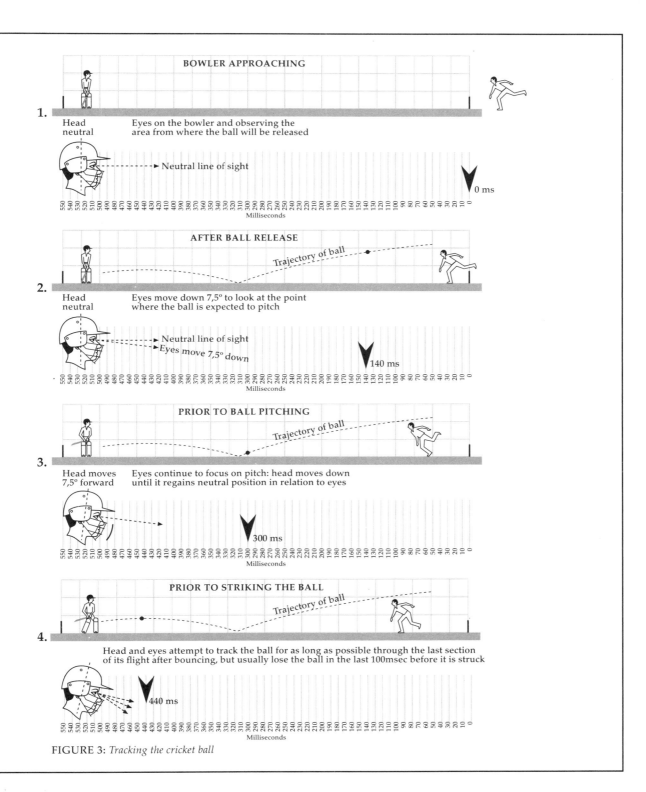

BOWLER APPROACHING

1.

Head neutral — Eyes on the bowler and observing the area from where the ball will be released

Neutral line of sight

0 ms

AFTER BALL RELEASE

Trajectory of ball

2.

Head neutral — Eyes move down 7,5° to look at the point where the ball is expected to pitch

Neutral line of sight

Eyes move 7,5° down

140 ms

PRIOR TO BALL PITCHING

Trajectory of ball

3.

Head moves 7,5° forward — Eyes continue to focus on pitch: head moves down until it regains neutral position in relation to eyes

300 ms

PRIOR TO STRIKING THE BALL

Trajectory of ball

4.

Head and eyes attempt to track the ball for as long as possible through the last section of its flight after bouncing, but usually lose the ball in the last 100msec before it is struck

440 ms

Milliseconds

FIGURE 3: *Tracking the cricket ball*

THE LIMITS OF REACTION TIME

Experiments like those reviewed on the previous pages have shown that batsmen tend to watch the bowler's arm and hand as he runs in, no doubt searching for some of the advance cues already mentioned. As the bowler braces into his delivery stride, the batsman performs a saccade from the bowler's hand to the area above and to the right (for a right-hand bowler) of the bowler's hand – in other words, the area from where he expects the ball to be released. Almost like a 'cut' in a film, the change of view is apparently instantaneous. As already outlined, the batsman then watches the delivery for a short time, but long enough to predict where the ball will pitch. Once he has made his decision, he performs another visual saccade, this time focusing on the place on the pitch where he has predicted the ball will land.

Figure 4 shows one of the crucial differences between good and great batters: because a batsman is unable to react to any deviation in the final 200 milliseconds of a delivery's flight, the earlier he can perform the saccade, the more swiftly and accurately he can respond to the delivery.

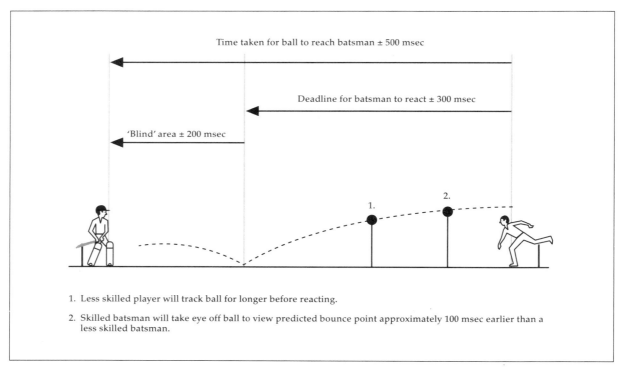

Time taken for ball to reach batsman ± 500 msec

Deadline for batsman to react ± 300 msec

'Blind' area ± 200 msec

1. Less skilled player will track ball for longer before reacting.
2. Skilled batsman will take eye off ball to view predicted bounce point approximately 100 msec earlier than a less skilled batsman.

FIGURE 4: *The visual responses (in milliseconds) of skilled and less skilled batters to the delivery of a good length ball. The more skilled batter will perform the saccade from the ball to the anticipated area it will pitch fractionally earlier.*

So why is the saccade an automatic reflex? Why do we make no conscious attempt to track the moving ball? The answer lies in the physiological limits of the human eye: we are physically unable to follow an object that requires our eyes to alter their angle of observation at more than 70° per second (Ripoll and Fleurance, 1988; Bahill and LaRitz, 1984). If anything moves across our field of vision at a greater speed, our brain takes control, predicting a point at which the object will appear in the immediate future, and performing a saccade to take the eyes to that point.

The ball has now landed, and the batsman watches it off the pitch, able to respond to any new visual information he might receive about deviation or bounce. But only up to a point: all batsmen have a point of no return, a point beyond which they are simply unable to respond to any late deviations (see Figure 5). The human nervous and muscular systems just don't move quickly enough. This also explains why fast bowlers are so feared, and why a delivery that pitches about 200 milliseconds before it reaches the batter is considered such a valuable one.

This frontier of reaction time, beyond which the batsman is more or less paralysed by our species' relatively lumbering reflexes, is found around 170 milliseconds before

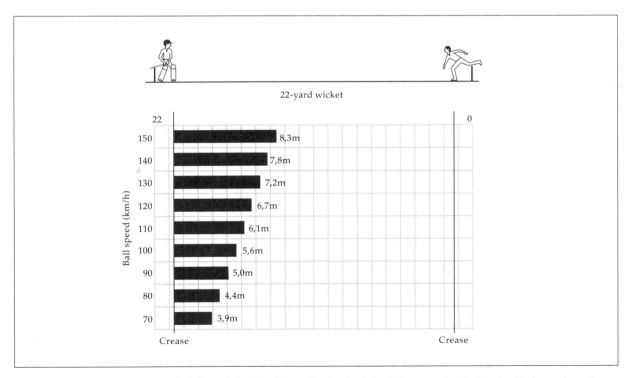

FIGURE 5: *This shows the distance the ball travels in 200 milliseconds when bowled at different speeds. The 'blind' or black area shows the distance the ball travels while the batter is still unable to 'compute' information and translate it into a new action.*

the ball reaches his hitting zone. Clearly, this refers to time rather than distance: 170 milliseconds against a pace bowler would leave the ball many metres further away from the bat than it would against a spin bowler. This figure – 170 milliseconds – has been termed 'one visual reaction time' (in other words, the smallest unit of reaction time) and was determined in a novel study conducted by Peter McLeod in Oxford in 1987.

He asked three English international batsmen, Wayne Larkins, Peter Willey and Allan Lamb, to bat on a matting wicket under which a series of wooden dowels, invisible to the batsmen, had been placed. Deliveries that pitched on flat matting naturally behaved predictably, coming through to the batsmen with only the conventional and expected deviations (bounce and negligible lateral movement). But balls that landed on one of the dowels deviated dramatically to either side. McLeod then filmed the batsmen, paying special attention to their reaction to these unexpected deviations – a hasty sideways movement of the bat in an effort to play the new line of the ball.

The conclusions were absolutely clear: under no circumstances was any batter able to adjust his stroke in less than about 170 milliseconds after the bounce of the ball. Thus McLeod (1987) concluded that 'one visual reaction time' is about 170 milliseconds. He further concluded, in line with legendary Australian spinner Clarrie Grimmett's suggestion, that a good length delivery should be defined as one which pitches too close to the batter for him to be able to respond to anything the delivery does off the pitch. Interestingly, in the late 1920s this was called a 'blind length' delivery.

Further study has slightly adjusted the above number: we now know that 200 milliseconds is the absolute cut-off period after which the batsman is hamstrung by his reactions. In other words: any delivery that makes an unpredictable movement less than 200 milliseconds from the batter is physically unplayable.

However, McLeod's findings raised an interesting question: how, he wondered, is it possible for a batsman to occupy the crease for hours on end without losing his wicket, when during that time he will receive perhaps a hundred or more 'unplayable' deliveries – in other words, balls that have pitched within 200 milliseconds of him?

He concluded that good batsmen, especially those facing quality bowlers able to make the ball deviate late, adopt two general strategies:
- They get as close to the pitch of the ball as possible, so that even if it deviates after pitching, it will not have moved far enough to beat the edge of the bat.
- They play defensive strokes with 'soft hands' (see p. 27), so that if the ball deviates and takes the edge, it will not have the momentum to reach fielders.

RAGE AGAINST THE DYING OF THE LIGHT

It has saved batsmen and Tests and enraged and enthralled spectators for generations. Despite rigorously policed schedules and over-rates, and multi-million dollar broadcasting deals, the modern game can still be brought to an abrupt halt by a batsman's inability (real or pretended!) to see through the gloom of an approaching evening. But why are batsmen 'offered the light'?

Fergus Campbell and colleagues (1987) from the University of Cambridge showed that reaction time becomes increasingly prolonged as the light fades beyond what is termed bright, and even before the light is perceived as 'dim'. They describe the conditions in the transition between bright and dim, as 'gloom'. The effect of gathering gloom on reaction time is dramatic. Luminance is measured on a log scale of 100 000 to $0cd/m^2$ (cd = candela, a unit of light), with $100 000cd/m^2$ being full light and $0cd/m^2$ complete darkness. Values of between 1 000 and $100cd/m^2$ represent light conditions described as 'gloom' – the point at which we begin to turn on car or house lights. It is within this range that human reaction time begins to slow. Campbell's study found that with each unit reduction in luminescence below bright light, human reaction time was reduced by 33 milliseconds. From a delivery from a fast bowler, this would translate into a travel distance of about 1 metre (another look at Figure 5 will remind us why 'gloom' is so potentially dangerous to batsmen).

This means that a batter would be less able to respond to a deviation in the ball's trajectory late in flight or after it pitched. The normal reaction time is about 170–200 milliseconds in good light, so that the batter is unable to respond to any deviation by the ball during the final 170–200 milliseconds of its flight. In bad light, the further slowing of reaction time means that the initial flight will take longer to detect, so that the batter will take longer to calculate the ball's trajectory. As a result, like Peter Kirsten batting in the dark, he will be less and less able to play attacking strokes, and will be forced to play defensively to those deliveries he did not 'see'. On top of this, he will be unable to respond to deviations in the ball's trajectory during the final 210 milliseconds of its flight, compared to 170–200 milliseconds in good light. So the bowler will be able to bowl shorter (by about a metre) and still have the ball treated as if it is of a 'good length'. Thus the bowler is able to be less accurate in his length while still curtailing scoring.

The biological explanation is that in bright light, the rod photoreceptors in the retina do not relay useful information to the brain. Cone receptors discriminate between colours in bright light, while rod cells are designed for black-and-white vision in poor light. The rods lack the discriminatory capacity of the cone cells, but as the light fades, they become increasingly active. It is assumed that the increasing activity of the rods cause this progressive delay in reaction time – they do not function as fast as do the cones.

THE VISUAL PITFALLS OF FLIGHT

The detection of the nature of a slow delivery requires visual and brain skills that are quite different to those required for predicting the future length and direction of a fast delivery. For example, a slow delivery may take about 900 milliseconds to reach the batsman. If the visual reaction time is 170 milliseconds and the movement time is 200 milliseconds, the batter still has nearly 600 milliseconds to observe the delivery before deciding how to play it.

But while he now has the luxury of being able to watch the ball for up to 600 milliseconds, he faces a new obstacle: flight.

For generations, spin bowlers have known that batsmen struggle against deliveries given plenty of 'air'. Common cricketing dogma has provided plenty of explanations for this phenomenon: the high trajectory forces the batsman to lift his head; the longer flight time allows the ball to spin and drift; the steep angle of descent will generate tricky bounce; and so on.

Certainly these factors might contribute to their fair share of dismissals, but the threat posed to batsmen by a looping delivery starts long before the ball drops onto the pitch and starts deviating away from the bat. It starts in his eyes; in an inherent weakness in his visual system. For the human brain is unable to predict the exact landing position of a delivery that, for a significant portion of its flight, moves above the horizontal direction of the gaze. (This suggests that instead of telling spinners to get the ball above the batsman's eyes, coaches should be telling them to get it above his eyes *for as long as possible*.)

In the case of a 'flighted' delivery, this is because during the early part of the ball's flight, its image on the retina provides only poor cues to the batsman as to exactly where the ball is in space, and therefore how far away from him it is, and how fast it is approaching (Regan, 1992; Regan, 1997). As a result, the batsman, while still able to predict accurately the exact arrival time of the ball, won't be certain of exactly where it will be in terms of its length at that moment (Regan, 1997).

While every ball delivered starts above the batter's horizontal eyeline, this weakness is not exploitable by fast bowlers, since the trajectory of a fast delivery will always be downwards from its point of release. This means that the batsman generally knows exactly from where in space a fast delivery will begin its descent.

Regan (1997) suggests that the slow bowler exploits this visual weakness in three ways: 'First, he delivers the ball in such a way as to prevent the batsman from predicting where the ball will hit the ground until it is too late to react correctly. Secondly, he forces the batsman to rely on the inadequate retinal image information obtained early in the ball's flight by delivering, with no discernible change in body posture or action, balls that dip or alternatively change direction after bouncing. Thirdly, over the course of several deliveries, he allows the batsman to learn a particular relationship between the early part of the ball's trajectory and the point where the ball hits the ground, and then changes the relationship with such art that the batsman does not detect the change' (pp. 550–51).

To study how and why good batsmen overcome these limitations, Renshaw and Fairweather (2000) tested their ability to detect the five different deliveries typically bowled by wrist spinners: off-breaks, leg-breaks, flippers, top-spin and back-spin.

They reasoned that a slow delivery bowled at 18m/s (65km/h) will take 200 milliseconds to travel 3,6 metres. Since, as has been explained, batsmen are likely to be unable to respond to any new information in the last 170–200 milliseconds of the delivery's trajectory, they will be unable to respond to the direction that the ball turns after pitching if the ball pitches 3,6 metres from the batsman – the definition of a good length delivery.

Since so many good deliveries from a bowler like Shane Warne pitch in this area, Renshaw and Fairweather concluded that skilled players of spin bowling must be able to predict the future direction of the spinning delivery on the basis of information detected from the bowler's action and updated during ball flight.

To evaluate this possibility, they used a temporal occlusion technique to evaluate the ability of different levels of batsmen to detect five different spinning deliveries under two conditions: (1) when they watched on videotape either the bowler's run-up and ball delivery throughout its flight up to the moment of ball contact; and (2) when only the bowler's run-up and the first 80 milliseconds of flight were shown, during which the ball would have travelled about 1,6 metres.

They showed that expert batters were better able to distinguish the different types of deliveries than less good players. They also found that for all groups, detection rates (percentage of deliveries correctly identified) were best for the leg-spin (90%) and googly (52%) deliveries, but were considerably less good for the flipper (32%), back-spin (23%) and top-spin (12%) deliveries. Surprisingly, viewing the full flight of the delivery did not add any further predictive value in the case of these deliveries. Hence predictions were equally good or poor (in the case of the flipper, back-spinner and top-spinner) regardless of whether only the delivery action and the first 1,6 metres of the flight were observed, or if the entire flight (approximately 15 metres) was viewed.

This study shows that essentially all the relevant information that the batter requires is provided in the spin bowler's action. Thus the batter makes his prediction of what the ball will do on the basis of advance cues in the delivery action. In addition, it seems that if the ball lands 3,8 metres or closer to the batsman, he is unable to play it 'off the pitch'. Rather he is playing it on the basis of his prediction made at the time of

The brain is unable to predict the exact landing position of a delivery that, for a significant portion of its flight, moves above the horizontal direction of the gaze. So instead of telling spinners to get the ball above the batsman's eyes, coaches should be telling them to get it above his eyes for as long as possible.

All the relevant information that the batter requires is provided in the spin bowler's action.

ball release. Of course, if the delivery is just short enough so that the batter can detect even a fraction of its trajectory after pitching, he will easily be able to play it 'off the pitch', placing it wherever his skill level will allow.

These authors also conclude that the more similar the bowler's action is when he delivers different deliveries, the greater the difficulty the batter will experience in detecting the nature of the delivery. This is why the leg-break and googly are more easily detected – they have the most distinctive delivery patterns and are also the most frequently bowled deliveries, so that batsmen are more used to playing and hence detecting them. In contrast, the delivery action for the flipper, back- and top-spinner deliveries are more similar, increasing the difficulty the batter will have in differentiating them. This has previously been shown in the detection rates for different tennis serves; it is more difficult to distinguish between those serves that are the most similar, for example, flat and slice serves (Goulet et al., 1989).

The authors make the compelling argument that all the information necessary to play each delivery is available to all batters and there is no time constraint when playing spin bowling. Thus those who are skilled at playing spin bowling are better able to extract that information. This comes through experience, but could clearly be enhanced by the use of video occlusion techniques. However, the focus should be on the bowler's action rather than on the delivery's subsequent trajectory. Meanwhile, the advice to bowlers is that they need to be taught to bowl many different deliveries from nearly identical actions.

In a follow-up study, Renshaw et al. studied the accuracy of prediction of batters facing the same five deliveries, but under visual occlusion conditions in which parts of the bowler's upper body anatomy were progressively removed from the video display. In the first condition, all the bowler's body parts were visible throughout the delivery stride; in the second condition, the bowler's arm and wrist were removed from the last delivery stride onwards; and in the third condition, the bowler's whole body was removed from the delivery stride, leaving only the ball visible during the delivery and flight phase. The authors found that for the leg-spin and the top-spin deliveries, there was no added advantage of seeing the bowling action – the flight alone allowed the batters to make similarly successful predictions. This is surprising, as it suggests that the leg-break delivery can be predicted with equal probability by detecting either advance cues, as discussed earlier, or by seeing only the flight of the delivery. This unexpected finding probably reflects the general familiarity that the batters have with facing leg-break bowlers.

In contrast, seeing only the flight reduced the accuracy of detecting the googly by about 50% to just over 20%; the flipper by about 30% from 35% to 25%; and the back-spin delivery also by more than 50%.

So the more complex slow deliveries that are bowled less frequently are detected with much greater difficulty. When facing those deliveries, the batter requires all the information available – both the bowler's action and the flight – to increase the probability of a successful prediction. But the probability of a successful detection remains rather low for the less-frequently bowled deliveries, and is almost no better than guess work.

One suggestion might be that bowlers should bowl these more complex deliveries more frequently, at least until the batters become as equally good at predicting those deliveries as they are at detecting leg-spin and googly deliveries. (Bowlers might disagree with this course of action!) Of course, it is not only the direction of turn that the bowler uses to deceive the batter. He must also be able, subtly, to alter the 'flight' of these different deliveries in order to extract the most from his art.

Another component of the superior performance of the elite becomes apparent when they process sports-specific visual information. In a classic study, Chase and Simon (1973) showed that experienced chess players were able to recall the positions of the chess pieces on the board with high levels of precision if the pieces had been left in place during the intermission of a real chess game. In contrast, if the pieces were randomly placed on the chessboard, experts were no better than novices in recalling the positions of the pieces. The explanation is that the experts recognized the pattern of play in the real game and thus could recall the position of the chess pieces on the basis of their historical knowledge of how that particular game was progressing at the time it was interrupted. By replaying the game in their brains, they were able more accurately to replace the pieces that had been removed from the real game (Allard et al., 1980).

Similarly, expert baseball and field hockey-players are better able to recall the positions of players when shown slides showing the development of a particular game situation. But without evidence that they could interpret as a developing play, they were no better than novices in recalling the exact positions of different players (Starkes, 1987). This is because expert players have a store of knowledge collected over the years they have played the game. They then compare any new information about a developing play with that old information in order to predict what is about to happen. In addition, they scan the playing field for the most relevant information, and use that information to make better predictions of what is about to happen than do novices.

In summary, these studies provide scientific proof for the contention made by Whiting in 1969 that: 'The expert will not only need to watch the ball for less of its flight, but he will also require less time to discriminate, programme and make decisions on the information that he receives' (p. 35).

SEEING RED: COLOUR-BLINDNESS AND CRICKETING ABILITY

As its name suggests, red-green colour-blindness affects the ability to see the colours red and green. Given that cricket involves a red ball leaping up off a green background, you would be forgiven for assuming that batsmen suffering from red-green colour-blindness are in for a rocky – and painful – ride.

To test this assumption, orthopaedic surgeon Nicholas Goddard (who himself suffers from red-green colour-blindness and a self-declared inability to strike the bowled cricket ball), and his colleague Dominic Coull, then at the Royal Free Hospital, London, tested 280 of the 306 professional cricketers who were playing county cricket in England in 1992.

They found that whereas 8% of the general population are colour-blind, only 4% of English professional cricketers are similarly affected. Was this the result of natural selection, with red-green colour-blind cricketers finding themselves disadvantaged and therefore less likely to turn professional? Perhaps. But the fact that there was still an appreciable number of red-green colour-blind first-class players suggests that this is a disability that can be overcome by cricketers.

In fact, the study found that the batting averages of those cricketers with red-green colour-blindness were no different from those with normal colour vision. Nor did the batting averages of colour-blind batters in one-day cricket improve after the white ball had been introduced into English Sunday League cricket, which might have been expected, given that the white ball is easier to pick up.

So it would seem that colour-blindness probably selects against a career in professional cricket; but those with red-green colour-blindness who do make it into professional cricket do not appear to be significantly disadvantaged, suggesting that they are able to compensate for what, superficially, would appear to be a significant disadvantage.

SUMMING UP

All cricketers need to understand that whatever mental activities of importance take place after a bowler begins his run-up occur in the primitive parts of the brain collectively known as the subconscious. The bowler cannot pitch the ball in a particular area through his conscious actions, just as the batter cannot execute a shot by thinking about it as he plays the shot. Nor can the fielder consciously decide how to catch a ball, whether it be a sharp chance in the slips or a high catch in the outfield that seems to hang in the heavens forever.

The best bowlers, batters and fielders in the world do everything better than their peers. But at the core of their success is the ability of their subconscious brains to process visual information, available to all, more accurately and more rapidly than others. They then use their superior motor skills to bat, bowl or field better than all others. But to allow their subconscious brains to do the job most effectively, all cricketers must resist the natural human response to believe that the conscious brain should be involved in the process. The brain hardware (or 'wetware') that evolved in our mammalian ancestors to control these responses developed long before the relatively new parts of our brains that control our thoughts and our ability to analyse events and draw conclusions. A monkey swinging gracefully at speed from the branches of one tree to the next does not stop to calculate the muscular forces needed to ensure that she reaches the branches of the next tree. She just lets it happen. If she had the higher brain functions found in modern human beings, she would realize that evolution had ensured that the basic motor functions necessary for her continued survival had been hardwired into the archaic parts of her brain millions of years earlier.

It is the descendants of these 'primitive' motor responses that allow cricketers to complete the extraordinary actions that they each do reflexively on the cricket field, *without* conscious thought.

It is important to grasp that cricketers perform best when they allow their subconscious brains to do those functions for which nature designed them, rather than crowding out reflexes – a result of the natural tendency of the conscious brain to take control.

So it is no wonder that cricketers, batters especially, perform best when they enter 'the zone'. In this state, their subconscious brains can best attend to the great visual and motor challenges posed by this unique game. Indeed, one of the fascinations of cricket is that it seems almost to have been designed to test the limits to which humans can develop these archaic brain systems.

SELECT BIBLIOGRAPHY

Abernethy, B. 1982. 'Skill in cricket batting: Laboratory and applied evidence.' *Proceedings of the Kinesiological Sciences Conference* 7: 35–50.

Abernethy, B. and D.G. Russell. 1984. 'Advance cue utilisation by skilled cricket batsmen.' *Australian Journal of Science and Medicine in Sport* 16 (2): 2–10.

Aginsky, K.D., et al. 2008. 'The detection of a throw.' *British Journal of Sports Medicine* (in press).

Akram, Wasim (with Patrick Murphy). 1998. *Akram: The Biography of Wasim Akram.* London: Piatkus.

Alexander, S., D. Underwood and A.J. Cooke. 1998. 'Cricket glove design' in *The Engineering of Sport: Design and Development*, ed. S.J. Haake. Oxford: Blackwell Science.

Alfred, Luke. 2001. *Lifting the Covers: The Inside Story of South African Cricket.* Cape Town: Spearhead.

Allsopp, P.E. 2005. *Measuring Team Performance and Modelling the Home Advantage Effect in Cricket.* PhD dissertation, Swinburne University of Technology, Australia.

Allsopp, P.E. and S.R. Clarke. 2004. 'Rating teams and analysing outcomes in one-day and Test cricket.' *Journal of the Royal Statistical Society: Series A* 167 (4): 657.

Andrew, Keith. 1986. *Coaching Cricket.* Ramsbury: The Crowood Press.

Arlott, John. 1949. *How to Watch Cricket.* London: Sporting Handbooks Ltd.

Arlott, John (ed). 1972. *Cricket: The Great Captains.* Newton Abbot: The Sportsmans Book Club.

Australian Cricket Board. 2000. *Coaching Youth Cricket.* Human Kinetics.

Bahill, A.T. and T. LaRitz. 1984. 'Why can't batters keep their eyes on the ball?' *American Scientist* 72: 249–253.

Barton, N.G. 1982. 'On the swing of a cricket ball in flight.' *Proceedings of the Royal Society of London: Series A* 379: 109–131.

Baum, Greg. 1996. 'What goes in to not getting out.' *The Good Weekend*, 21 December: 26–33.

Bawden, Mark and Ian Maynard. 2001. 'Towards an understanding of the personal experience of the "yips" in cricket.' *Journal of Sports Sciences* 19 (12): 937–53.

Bell-Jenje, T.C. and J. Gray. 2005. 'Incidence, nature and risk factors in shoulder injuries of national academy cricket players over 5 years – a retrospective study.' *South African Journal of Sports Medicine* 17 (4): 22–28.

Benaud, Richie. 1998. *Anything But … An Autobiography.* London: Hodder & Stoughton.

Botham, Ian (with Peter Hayter). 1995. *My Autobiography – Don't Tell Kath.* London: CollinsWillow.

Bradman, Donald. 1958. *The Art of Cricket.* London: Hodder & Stoughton.

Brearley, Mike. 1985. *The Art of Captaincy.* London and Sydney: Hodder & Stoughton.

Broadstock, M. 1991. 'Sun protection at the cricket.' *Medical Journal of Australia* 154 (6): 430.

Brooks, R.D., R.W. Faff and D. Sokulsky. 2002. 'An ordered response model of Test cricket performance.' *Applied Economics* 34 (18).

Burnett, A.F., M.S. Khangure et al. 1996. 'Thoracolumbar disc degeneration in young fast bowlers in cricket: A follow-up study.' *Clinical Biomechanics* 11 (6): 305–310.

Campbell, F.W., S.E. Rothwell et al. 1987. 'Bad lights stops play.' *Ophthalmic & Physiological Optics: The Journal of the British College of Ophthalmic Opticians (Optometrists)* 7 (2): 165–67.

Cardus, Neville. 1929. *The Summer Game.* London: Grant Richards & Humphrey Toulmin.

Carter, M. and G. Guthrie. 2004. 'Cricket interruptus: Fairness and incentive in limited overs cricket matches.' *The Journal of the Operational Research Society* 55: 822–29.

Chappell, Greg. 2004. *Cricket: The Making of Champions.* South Melbourne: Lothian Books.

Cheetham, Jack. 1956. *I Declare.* Cape Town: Howard Timmins.

Christie, C.J., L. Todd and G.A. King. 2003. 'Energy cost of batting during a simulated cricket work bout.' In *Science and Medicine in Cricket*, eds. R.A. Stretch, T.D. Noakes and C.L. Vaughan, Second World Congress of Science and Medicine in Cricket.

Clarke, S.R. and P.E. Allsopp. 2001. 'Fair measures of performance: The World Cup of cricket.' *The Journal of the Operational Research Society* 52 (4): 471–79.

Clarke, S.R. and J.M. Norman. 1999. 'To run or not?: Some dynamic programming models in cricket.' *The Journal of the Operational Research Society* 50 (5): 536–545.

Clarke, S.R. and J.M. Norman. 2003. 'Dynamic programming in cricket: Choosing a night watchman.' *The Journal of the Operational Research Society* 54: 838–45.

Constantine, Learie (with C.L.R. James). 1933. *Cricket and I*. London: Allan.

Constantine, Learie (with Denzil Batchelor). 1966. *The Changing Face of Cricket*. London: Eyre & Spottiswoode.

Cook, Geoff and Neville Scott. 1991. *The Narrow Line: An Anatomy of Professional Cricket*. London: The Kingswood Press.

Cooke, J.C. 1955. 'The boundary layer and "seam" bowling.' *The Mathematical Gazette*: 196–99.

Daish, C.B. 1972. *The Physics of Ball Games*. London: The English Universities Press Ltd.

Dellor, Ralph. 1990. *How to Coach Cricket*. London: Willow Books.

De Moore, G.M. 1999. 'The suicide of Thomas Wentworth Wills.' *Medical Journal of Australia* 171 (11–12): 656–58.

De Silva, B.M. and T.B. Swartz. 1997. 'Winning the coin toss and the home team advantage in one-day international cricket matches.' *The New Zealand Statistician* 32: 16–22.

De Villiers, R.V., M. Pritchard et al. 2005. 'Scapular stress fracture in a professional cricketer and a review of the literature.' *South African Medical Journal* 95 (5): 312–317.

Donald, Allan (with Patrick Murphy). 2000. *White Lightning: The Autobiography*. Johannesburg: Jonathan Ball Publishers in conjunction with CollinsWillow.

Duckworth, F.C. and A.J. Lewis. 2004. 'A successful operational research intervention in one-day cricket.' *The Journal of the Operational Research Society* 55: 749–59.

Fingleton, J.H. 1946. *Cricket Crisis: Body Line and Other Lines*. Melbourne: Cassell & Co. Ltd.

Fletcher, J.G. 1955. 'Calories and cricket.' *Lancet* 268 (6 875): 1 165–66.

Francis, Tony. 1992. *The Zen of Cricket: Learning from Positive Thought*. London: Hutchinson.

Frith, David. 1990. *By His Own Hand: A Study of Cricket's Suicides*, republished as *Silence of the Heart: Cricket Suicides* in 2001. Edinburgh: Mainstream Publishers.

Fry, C.B. 1912. *Cricket (Batsmanship)*. London: Everleigh Nash & Co.

Gilfillan, T.C. and N. Nobandla. 2000. 'Modelling the performance of the South African national cricket team.' *South African Journal for Research in Sport, Physical Education and Recreation* 22 (1): 97–110.

Glazier, P.S., G.P. Paradisis et al. 2000. 'Anthropometric and kinematic influences on release speed in men's fast-medium bowling.' *Journal of Sports Sciences* 18 (12): 1 013–21.

Goddard, N. and D. Coull. 1994. 'Colour-blind cricketers and snowballs.' *British Medical Journal* 309 (6 970): 1 684–85.

Gore, C.J., P.C. Bourdon et al. 1993. 'Involuntary dehydration during cricket.' *International Journal of Sports Medicine* 14 (7): 387–95.

Goulet, C., C. Bard et al. 1989. 'Expertise Differences in Preparing to Return a Tennis Serve: A Visual Information Processing Approach.' *Journal of Sport and Exercise Psychology* 11: 382–98.

Gregory, P.L., M.E. Batt et al. 2004. 'Comparing spondylolysis in cricketers and soccer players.' *British Journal of Sports Medicine* 38 (6): 737–742.

Grimmett, Clarence. 1934. *Tricking the Batsman*. London: Hodder & Stoughton.

Guha, Ramachandra. 1994. *Spin and Other Turns*. New Delhi and London: Penguin.

Hardcastle, P.H. 1993. 'Repair of spondylolysis in young fast bowlers.' *Journal of Bone and Joint Surgery (British Volume)* 75 (3): 398–402.

Hoberman, J. 1992. *Mortal Engines: The Science of Performance and the Dehumanization of Sport.* New York: The Free Press.

Holmes, Richard. 2003. *Acts of War: The Behaviour of Men in Battle.* London: Weidenfeld & Nicholson.

Hughes, Simon. 1997. *A Lot of Hard Yakka.* London: Headline.

Hughes, Simon. 2001. *Jargonbusting: The Analyst's Guide to Test Cricket.* London: Channel Four Books / Macmillan.

Humphries, D. and M. Jamison. 2004. 'Clinical and magnetic resonance imaging features of cricket bowler's side strain.' *British Journal of Sports Medicine* 38 (5): E21.

James, C.L.R. 1963, 1994. *Beyond A Boundary.* London: Serpent's Tail.

Johnstone, P.G. 2003. '"Sledging" – the practice of psychological distraction in cricket.' In *Science and Medicine in Cricket,* eds. R.A. Stretch, T.D. Noakes and C.L. Vaughan, Second World Congress of Science and Medicine in Cricket.

Kantor, Brian. 2007. 'A statistical analysis of the World Cup 2007.' Investec Newsletter 11 May.

Keri, J., et al. 2006. *Baseball Between the Numbers.* New York: Basic Books.

Kimber, A.C. and A.R. Hansford. 1993. 'A statistical analysis of batting in cricket.' *Journal of the Royal Statistical Society Series A: Statistics in Society* 156 (3): 443–55.

Kirk, D., T. Carlson et al. 1997. 'The economic impact on families of children's participation in junior sport.' *Australian Journal of Science and Medicine in Sport* 29 (2): 27–33.

Knott, Alan. 1977. *Wicket-keeping.* London: Stanley Paul.

Lamb, Allan (with Jack Bannister). 1997. *Allan Lamb: My Autobiography.* London: CollinsWillow.

Land, M.F. and P. McLeod. 2000. 'From eye movements to actions: how batsmen hit the ball.' *Nature Neuroscience* 3 (12): 1 340–45.

Lara, Brian (with Brian Scovell). 1994. *Brian Lara: Beating the Field.* London: Partridge Press.

Lewis, Michael. 2003. *Moneyball: The Art of Winning an Unfair Game.* New York: W.W. Norton & Company.

Lewis, Tony. 1994. *MCC Masterclass: The New MCC Coaching Book.* London: Weidenfeld & Nicolson.

Lillee, Dennis (with Bob Harris). 2003. *Lillee: An Autobiography.* Sydney: Hodder.

Lyttleton, R.A. 1957. 'The swing of a cricket ball.' *Cricket Journal:* 186–191.

Marshall, R. and R. Ferdinands. 2003. 'The effect of a flexed elbow on bowling speed in cricket.' *Sports Biomechanics* 2 (1): 65–71.

Martin-Jenkins, Christopher. 1996. *World Cricketers: A Biographical Dictionary.* Oxford: Oxford University Press.

May, Peter. 1956. *Peter May's Book of Cricket.* London: Cassell and Company Ltd.

McLeod, Peter. 1987. 'Visual reaction time and high speed ball games.' *Perception* 16 (1): 49–59.

Mehta, R.D. 1985. 'Aerodynamics of sports balls.' *Annual Review of Fluid Mechanics* 17: 151–189.

Mehta, R.D. and D. Wood. 1980. 'Aerodynamics of the cricket ball.' *New Scientist:* 442–47.

Mehta, R.D, K. Bentley et al. 1983. 'Factors affecting cricket ball swing.' *Nature* 303 (30 June 1983): 787–88.

Milburn, P.D. and G. Nuttridge. 1999. *The Nature, Prevalence and Risk Factors Associated with Pace Bowling Injuries in Men's Cricket.* Wellington: Sports Science New Zealand Technical Report.

Noakes, T.D. 2006. 'Laboratory research, commercial interests and advice to the public on fluid ingestion during exercise: The development of a fatal foundation myth.' *Clinical Journal of*

Sport Medicine (submitted).

Noakes, T.D. 2003. 'Overconsumption of fluids by athletes.' *British Medical Journal* 327 (7 407): 113–114.

Noakes, T.D. 2003. *Lore of Running* (4th edition). Cape Town: Oxford University Press.

Noakes, T.D., N. Goodwin et al. 2005. 'Water intoxication: a possible complication during endurance exercise.' *Wilderness and Environmental Medicine* 16 (4): 221–27.

Noakes, T.D. and S. Granger. 1995. *Running Your Best*. Cape Town: Oxford University Press.

Noakes, T.D. and A. St Clair Gibson. 2004. 'Logical limitations to the "catastrophe" models of fatigue during exercise in humans.' *British Journal of Sports Medicine* 38 (5): 648–49.

Noakes, T.D., A. St Clair Gibson et al. 2004. 'From catastrophe to complexity: a novel model of integrative central neural regulation of effort and fatigue during exercise in humans.' *British Journal of Sports Medicine* 38 (4): 511–14.

Noakes, T.D., A. St Clair Gibson et al. 2005. 'From catastrophe to complexity: a novel model of integrative central neural regulation of effort and fatigue during exercise in humans: summary and conclusions.' *British Journal of Sports Medicine* 39 (2): 120–24.

Nummela, A.T., K.A. Heath et al. 2008. 'Fatigue during a 5-km running time trial.' *International Journal of Sports Medicine* (in press).

Orchard, J., T. James et al. 2002. 'Injuries in Australian cricket at first-class level 1995/1996 to 2000/2001.' *British Journal of Sports Medicine* 36 (4): 270–74.

Oslear, Don and Jack Bannister. 1996. *Tampering With Cricket*. London: CollinsWillow.

Peebles, Ian. 1969. *Straight From the Shoulder: 'Throwing' – its History and Cure*. Newton Abbot: The Sportsmans Book Club.

Penrose, J.M.T. and N.K. Roach. 1995. 'Decision-making and advanced cue utilisation by cricket batsmen.' *Journal of Human Movement Studies* 29: 199–218.

Potter, Jack and Ashley Mote. 2001. *The Winning Edge: The Secrets and Techniques of the World's Best Cricketers*. Manchester: The Parrs Wood Press.

Ranawat, V.S., J.K. Dowell et al. 2003. 'Stress fractures of the lumbar pars interarticularis in athletes: a review based on long-term results of 18 professional cricketers.' *Injury* 34 (12): 915–919.

Ranjitsinhji, K.S. 1897. *The Jubilee Book of Cricket*. Edinburgh and London: William Blackwood.

Regan, D. 1992. 'Visual judgements and misjudgements in cricket, and the art of flight.' *Perception* 21 (1): 91–115.

Regan, D. 1997. 'Visual factors in hitting and catching.' *Journal of Sports Sciences* 15 (6): 533–58.

Renshaw, I. and M.M. Fairweather. 2000. 'Cricket bowling deliveries and the discrimination ability of professional and amateur batters.' *Journal of Sports Sciences* 18 (12): 951–57.

Richards, Viv (with Bob Harris). 2000. *Sir Vivian: The Definitive Autobiography*. London: Michael Joseph.

Riley, Pat. 1994. *The Winner Within: A Life Plan for Team Players*. Berkley Trade.

Ripoll, H. and P. Fleurance. 1988. 'What does keeping one's eye on the ball mean?' *Ergonomics* 31 (11): 1 647–54.

Rundell, Michael. 1996. *The Dictionary of Cricket*. Oxford: Oxford University Press.

Sharwood, K.A., M. Collins et al. 2004. 'Weight changes, medical complications, and performance during an Ironman triathlon.' *British Journal of Sports Medicine* 38 (6): 718–724.

Scarf, P. and X. Shi. 2005. 'Modelling match outcomes and decision support for setting a final innings target in test cricket.' *IMA Journal of Management Mathematics* 16 (2): 161–78.

Shillinglaw, A.L. 2003. *Bradman Revisited: The Legacy of Sir Donald Bradman*. Manchester: The Parrs Wood Press.

Simpson, Bob (with Terry Brindle). 1996. *The Reasons Why*. Sydney: HarperSports.

Sobers, Garfield (with Ivo Tennant). 1996. *Sobers: The Changing Face of Cricket*. London: Ebury Press.

St Clair Gibson, A., E.V. Lambert et al. 2001. 'Exercise and fatigue-control mechanisms.' *International Journal of Sports Medicine* 2 (3): 1–14.

Stretch, R.A., G. Barnard et al. 2002. 'Improving the accuracy and consistency of shot reproduction in cricket batting through a vision training programme.' *The South African Optometrist* 61 (4): 145–150.

Stretch, R.A. 2003. 'Cricket injuries: a longitudinal study of the nature of injuries to South African cricketers.' *British Journal of Sports Medicine* 37 (3): 250–253.

Stretch, R.A., R. Bartlett et al. 2000. 'A review of batting in men's cricket.' *Journal of Sports Sciences* 18 (12): 931–49.

Stretch, R.A., E. du Toit et al. 1998. 'The force absorption characteristics of cricket batting pads at four impact velocities.' *Sports Medicine* (October 1998): 9–13.

Stretch, R.A. and J. Tyler. 1995. 'The force absorption characteristics of cricket batting gloves at four impact velocities.' *Sports Medicine* (September 1995): 22–29.

Stretch, R.A., J.V. von Hagen et al. 2000. 'The effect of fencamfamine on the accuracy and consistency of shot reproduction in cricket batting.' *Sports Medicine* (November 2000): 21–25.

Swartz, T.B., P.S. Gill et al. 2006. 'Optimal batting orders in one-day cricket.' *Comparative and Operational Research* 33: 1939–50.

Synge, Allen and Derek Anns. 1987. *Masterstrokes*. London: The Kingswood Press.

Tainton, Neil and John Klug. 2002. *The Cricket Pitch and its Outfield*. Pietermaritzburg: University of Natal Press.

Tucker, R., L. Rauch et al. 2004. 'Impaired exercise performance in the heat is associated with an anticipatory reduction in skeletal muscle recruitment.' *Pflugers Archive* 448 (4): 422–430.

Turner, Matthew. 2002. *The Motion of Balls in Sports*. Dept of Mathematics, University of East Anglia.

Tyson, Frank. 1977. *Complete Cricket Coaching*. London: Pelham Books Ltd.

Warne, Shane (with Mark Ray). 1997. *My Own Story*. London: Bookman Projects Ltd.

Waugh, Steve. 1995. *Steve Waugh's West Indies Tour Diary*. Sydney: HarperSports.

Webster, F.A.M. 1948. *The Science of Athletics*. London: Nicholas Kaye.

Williams, Charles. 1997. *Bradman: An Australian Hero*. London: Abacus.

Woolmer, Bob. 1984. *Bob Woolmer: Pirate and Rebel? An Autobiography*. London: Arthur Barker Ltd.

Woolmer, Bob. 1993. *Skilful Cricket*. London: A & C Black.

Woolmer, Bob (with Ivo Tennant). 2000. *Woolmer on Cricket*. London: Virgin Publishing Ltd.

INDEX

Note: page numbers in *italic* refer to illustrations or examples.